BETTE DAVIS

Biography

A Screen Legend's Story

Ardyce R Dietz

Copyright © 2023
All rights reserved

The content of this book may not be reproduced, duplicated, or transmitted without the author's or publisher's express written permission. Under no circumstances will the publisher or author be held liable or legally responsible for any damages, reparation, or monetary loss caused by the information contained in this book, whether directly or indirectly.

Legal Notice:
This publication is copyrighted. It is strictly for personal use only. You may not change, distribute, sell, use, quote, or paraphrase any part of this book without the author's or publisher's permission.

Disclaimer Notice:
Please keep in mind that the information in this document is only for educational and entertainment purposes. Every effort has been made to present accurate, up-to-date, reliable, and comprehensive information. There are no express or implied warranties. Readers understand that the author is not providing legal, financial, medical, or professional advice. This book's content was compiled from a variety of sources. Please seek the advice of a licensed professional before attempting any of the techniques described in this book. By reading this document, the reader agrees that the author is not liable for any direct or indirect losses incurred as a result of using the information contained within this document, including, but not limited to, errors, omissions, or inaccuracies.

TABLE OF CONTENTS

1. Spawned in Witch Country

2. Struggling to the Surface

3. Hollywood

4. Warner, Zanuck-and Arliss

5. Ham, Sex, and Other Things

6. Battling Toward the Big Break

7. Of Human Bondage-and Recognition

8. Grinding out the Warner Sausage

9. The First Oscar-and Its Aftermath

10. The Great Rebellion-and the Return

11. Bette O'Hara?

12. 1939: The Great Year

13. A Legend-But Alone

14. The Lioness in Winter

1.

Spawned in Witch Country

On April 5, 1908, Ruth Elizabeth Davis was born in the mill town of Lowell, Massachusetts. There was much hype afterward to the effect that she had made her debut in a flurry of lightning and thunder, but it was actually a day of mild breeze and a little rain. Despite the fact that the city was primarily an industrial one, with textile workers continually on strike and nasty worker-police clashes on the streets on a regular basis, Davis was from one of the "old families." She was born in the upper-class Chester Street home of her maternal grandmother. Harlow Morrell Davis, her father, was a young Bates College graduate who went on to Harvard Law School and became a successful patent lawyer and government consultant. He was a descendant of Welch James Davis, who came to New England in 1634 and helped create the town of Haverhill. Her mother, Ruth Favour, was descended from seventeenth-century English and Huguenot settlers. The Huguenot Favors had mingled their blood so thoroughly with the old Brahmins that they were pure bluebloods. There was even a Salem witch in the family line.

Her father was a cold, unemotional, distant guy, while her mother, whom she always referred to as "Ruthie," was a lady who lived in her emotions. They were an odd, mismatched couple. They divorced when "Betty" (Betty with a y) was seven and her younger sister Barbara (named Bobby) was six. Three years later, in 1918, came a full-fledged divorce, which shocked all their staid, proper family at an era when divorce was nearly synonymous with immorality.

She later recalled that during her first seven years of life, she "could not recall one moment of affection between my parents." Davis was deeply affected by this unloving marriage, despite being treated well by her mother's relatives and having all of the needs. "I was fed impermanence and insecurity," she explained. Men made promises they didn't keep. They abandoned women, just like my father abandoned my mother. Nothing endured, not even love or life itself. One lived day by day. One made due, savouring the occasion. The past was unrecoverable. The future presented a challenge and a risk."

She had a rough start with her father at the beginning—the very beginning. On July 1, 1907, he married her mother, and she arrived nine months later, almost to the day. Her father had not anticipated having a child so soon. His studies and tight budget did not allow for it. He tried to persuade her mother to have an abortion, which appalled Ruth's brother, an Episcopal preacher. Harlow Morrell Davis was a pragmatist and an atheist. He was dealing with facts. The rest was romantic nonsense. He later punished Betty with unloving coldness and indifference for his decision to end Betty's life before it had even begun. Davis would have this attitude toward both of his daughters for the rest of his life.

Unwanted-and then abandoned-by the first guy in her life, Betty-later re-spelled Bette because a friend of her mother's had read Balzac's Cousin Bette and thought the e at the end sounded more glamorous and actress-like-developed a distrust of men that lasted her entire life. "Childhood reveals the adult," as an old adage goes. Because of the emotional traumas inflicted on his two daughters by Harlow Morrell Davis, Bette came to see men as rivals to be defeated, whereas Bobby saw them as terrifying threats. Bette Davis noted many years later, following her fourth and final divorce, "I always knew I would end up an old woman alone on a hill."

During her mother's marriage to Davis, Ruthie was a loving flibbertigibbet of a woman, childlike and feminine. She appeared to her relatives and friends to be all sweetness and light, devoted to her children and meticulous in her maternal duties. However, appearances can be deceiving. Her husband's abandonment and divorce in 1918 brought the true woman to the fore. She imagined herself and her two children as the Three Musketeers, Three Against the World, iron-willed survivors, come what may.

Bette's feelings toward her younger sister Bobby were always ambiguous. Bobby felt neglected, almost unloved, as she basked in her mother's adoration, certain that Ruthie saw her as the talent to be cultivated, the white hope. Bobby had always felt inferior to Bette in terms of appearance, intelligence, and artistic ability. Bobby failed in all of her personal and professional endeavours because she lacked her mother's and sister's strong ego and determination to survive. Her emotions of inferiority evolved into mental disease, which waxed and waned like a recurring fever.

Harlow Morrell Davis left Ruthie with alimony that was hardly enough to cover her basic needs, despite the fact that he was a successful patent lawyer. Ruthie demonstrated the genuine mettle of her sturdy Huguenot and Yankee ancestors by going to work as a housekeeper and a dormitory mother in various colleges after a few ill-advised and futile attempts to gain more money from her parsimonious ex-spouse. This woman, who loved art and music, was a photographer, painter, and a great public speaker, was not arrogant. She took every job that came her way and fit her immediate requirements, and she taught Bette that a person should be assessed not by the job she had, but by who she demonstrated herself to be—that was where true dignity rested. Bette later worked as a waitress to supplement her income while attending an academy.

Ruthie and her two girls had no choice but to go where the work was. It was sometimes New York City. It was sometimes Boston, Newton, Massachusetts, or Maine. Bette Davis subsequently estimated that they had lived in approximately 75 apartments, furnished rooms, or houses between 1918 and 1926.

Bette Davis realised that life was a war throughout those years, from the age of 10 to sixteen. Everything had to be fought for. Fight for your self-esteem. Fight for survival, because the male was more hazardous than the most fearsome tiger or bird. Ruthie taught Bette that women have to look after themselves. Harlow Morrell Davis had been willing to be her homemaker, helpmeet, faithful and loving little wife for the rest of her life, but he had ripped the rug out from under her. Okay, if males were like that, she'd be tough and self-sufficient.

Thirty years later, young Barbara Davis Sherry heard echoes of that long-ago refrain from her mother, the world-famous film star: Men were untrustworthy, and love lasted only a short time. Men went roving after the initial sexual thrill and romance had worn off, looking for something or someone new, fresh, and exciting. Men desired change and lacked consistency. They were icy, authoritarian, and ruthless. Women must always remain vigilant.

After attending public schools in Lowell and Winchester, Massachusetts, the Davis daughters were moved to Crestalban, a remote academy in the Berkshires that fostered outdoor activities and wholesome hobbies. Ruthie ensured that her girls were dressed properly by working as a governess for various wealthy households, but they were painfully aware that other children had prosperous fathers and loving, intact homes, with all the snug comforts and securities that entailed. Bobby's reaction was to withdraw into her own world. Bette reacted by participating in school performances and contending for prizes. She was dead set on being the best, the biggest, and the brightest. She longed for the day when Ruthie would no longer have to work so hard, when she would be the sole provider.

Davis came too close to a Christmas tree while playing Santa Claus at Crestalban and suffered serious facial burns that burned severely. Her skin's outer layer had to be removed, and she suffered for months as her mother oiled her face continually. The skin recovered thanks to proper care, but with the outer layer lacking, it was sensitive to the sun, harsh cosmetics, and other irritants. Although her vision was unaffected, her blue eyes became noticeable because she bulged them outward compensatorily to reassure herself that they were still functional.

The Davises moved frequently during Bette's high school years, from 1922 to 1926. Ruthie took the girls to live in a one-room Upper West Side apartment while working in a photographic studio in New York. They later relocated to East Orange, New Jersey, where Davis recalls a gloomy small flat with a cramped, drab atmosphere. The sisters then returned to Newton, Massachusetts, where they attended the local high school. Bette and Bobby ended up at Cushing Academy in Ashburnham, Massachusetts, where Bette spent her junior and senior years.

When they met in 1924, Davis was sixteen and Henry Fonda was nineteen. Davis developed a crush on Hank while on a double date with a friend and her sister, which was not returned. He later claimed that soon she was out of sight, he forgot about her. She appears to have carried a torch for several months, penning him letters that he did not bother to respond to. They wouldn't see each other again for another thirteen years, and then under very different circumstances.

Bette attracted a lot of beaux during her geographical and scholastic wanderings, most of whom she kept at a friendly distance. Ruthie, who held staunchly puritanical views about the opposite sex, instilled in the girls that losing virginity before marriage was the worst thing that could happen to a woman. She asserted that boys and men were passionate, driven beings, slaves of their sexual desires; they sought only to please themselves, leaving the consequences-venereal disease, pregnancy, loss of reputation and self-esteem-on their hapless female partners of the moment. Ruthie explained to the girls that a woman's virginity was her integrity, her armour, and her shield against the rampaging, predatory male. Retain it, and men will respect her from a safe distance; surrender it, and they will treat her as a toy to be discarded. entire love and entire surrender could only be found in marriage-and even that required a cautious, deliberate approach.

The girls' reactions to this counsel varied according to their personalities: To the unstable, frail Bobby, it represented dread and distrust of the masculine, whereas to the self-assured, strong Bette, it meant aggression, challenge, and role-playing.

The shy, gangling Harmon Oscar "Ham" Nelson, who was a year ahead of her at Cushing Academy, was the first guy to get through Bette Davis's emotional defences but not physically (she remained a virgin until she ultimately married him at twenty-four). His sensitive essence appealed to Bette, bringing out a maternal and protecting element in her. He was big, gawky, awkward, with liquid brown eyes and a broad nose. Her essential opinions toward males became clear in her sixteenth year. Ham was too frail to pose a danger, and he appeared to be questioning his masculinity. He never made passes at her, never tried to be alone with her, never pawed her, never manipulated her for kisses. She wished he would at times. He was cast in character roles rather than romantic lead roles in plays with her. Davis would watch her bashful swain nervously tinkling on his piano or tooting his trumpet in the school ensemble. Despite his talent as a musician, she treated him with caution and scorn. This was no handsome Sir Galahad eager to sweep her off her feet, no commanding masculine willing to aggressively pitch for what he desired. Although she liked Ham, a part of her wished to be completely feminine, surrendering, and dominated by a guy she could like and respect.

Bette Davis's personality was torn between a desire for a powerful guy to whom she could commit herself without reservation and a desire for weak, clinging, docile males.

Meanwhile, at Cushing, Davis benefited from the guidance of such outstanding dramatic coaches as Lois Cann, who taught her a unique sort of expressionism—a dynamic, disciplined projective method that she adopted into her acting permanently. She appeared in several school plays at Cushing, including Booth Tarkington's Seventeen. Ham played a supporting part in this. She missed him when he graduated a year ahead of her in the class of 1925. Ham embarked on an uncertain career. After attending an agricultural college and performing some band work, he ended up at Amherst. He finally graduated at the ripe (for college) age of twenty-five, after which he spent his time playing in bands. He and Bette stayed in touch over the years, meeting when their schedules allowed. Ruthie liked him because his family was right, his Yankee heritage was right, and most importantly, he was gentle and manageable, a kind, affectionate puppy dog in her opinion. She wanted a man like that for her girls. It was assumed that no matter how much Bette wandered in the male woodlands, Ham was the man she would eventually marry.

Davis travelled with her mother to Peterborough, New Hampshire, during the summer between her junior and senior years, where Ruthie had found work as a photographer. At her mother's advice, she enrolled in a dancing school that also offered acting classes. Mariarden was the name of the school. While there, she was influenced by a dancing teacher who dubbed herself Roshanara, despite her origins being plebeian English. Roshanara was a self-made woman who had transformed her life into "a thing of beauty, glamour, and elegance." Davis credits Roshanara with teaching her the grace of movement that she eventually used in acting.

Bette, then seventeen, performed in an outdoor play of A Midsummer Night's Dream while at Mariarden that summer of 1925. Frank Conroy, a seasoned Broadway and classical actor who subsequently became a notable character actor in talking pictures, directed it. Conroy first observed her here, and he was even more captivated by her in The Moth, another show in which Roshanara cast her. She danced the title role with such grace and style that

Conroy told her mother, "That girl needs to be an actress." You can't take your gaze away from her because she exudes a radiance that is uniquely hers. She has a place on the stage and nowhere else."

Davis graduated from Cushing Academy in 1926, her future uncertain despite Conroy's encouraging remarks. She worked as a secretary and other odd jobs since she felt she had become too much of a burden to her mother. Ruthie treated her to a theatre trip to Boston a few months later. There she saw Henrik Ibsen's touching and powerful The Wild Duck, starring Blanche Yurka, a noted stage actress with wild eyes and a flashing, driving style, and Peg Entwistle, a sensitive young actress of great promise who jumped to her death from one of the HOLLYWOOD sign's mammoth letters in the 1930s. Seeing the shows, she said, had strengthened her resolve to become an actress. She couldn't be happy any other way, she informed her mother. She stated she needed to cleanse intense, stormy, elemental feelings inside of her, and acting was the only way to do it.

Ruthie accompanied Davis (Bobby was at school) to New York in the fall of 1927, convinced that Bette's future rested in acting and that all other endeavours must be subordinated to that purpose. One of the country's most brilliant and recognized actresses, Eva Le Gallienne, had formed the Civic Repertory Theatre, which offered modestly priced tickets and well-directed, well-acted interpretations of the classics on a shoestring budget. Miss Le Gallienne was a diligent technician and a strict perfectionist who insisted on high standards, even for newbies. She was charitable and dedicated to supporting young talent. She wasn't taken with the young Bette Davis. Bette flubbed and bungled her way through a part that was beyond her ability at the moment, that of an elderly woman, with terrible results. Years later, she said that if she sensed someone did not like her or was against her from the start, she froze. When Miss Le Gallienne pointed out problems in her trial interpretation, Davis upset the Great Lady by stating that she was a beginner, not an accomplished technician, and that she had come to study, not to display.

Le Gallienne, mistaking Davis's humility for pride, calmly informed the aspirant that she would hear from her via letter. The harsh verdict arrived about a week later. It was something along the lines of Bette Davis not displaying a serious or professional approach to her would-be job to merit bringing her on.

When asked about it many years later, Eva Le Gallienne shrugged and said, "So many young people came down to Fourteenth Street back then, hoping and seeking." I simply don't recall her."

Davis, crushed by the rejection, mooned around the house in Newton, Massachusetts, where she, Ruthie, and Bobby were residing at the time. Bobby decided to attend college in the Midwest about this time. She had the distinct impression that she had been forgotten, and that all bets were, as usual, on Bette. Davis went on to say, years later, "I don't blame her for beating a retreat to someplace far away where, for a while anyway, she could feel like her own person."

Then Ruthie had another thought. She and Bette took the train back to New York, this time to the Robert Milton-John Murray Anderson School of the Theatre. They had been disheartened by a letter from Harlow Morrell Davis, who despised Bette as an actor, just before leaving Boston. "She doesn't have what it takes." She should be sensible and look for work as a secretary."

Ignoring her father's disapproval, Ruthie marched inside the school and told the director, "My girl wants to be an actress." She has a lot of talent. Frank Conroy believes she has limitless potential. I don't have the funds to pay your tuition, but would you kindly accept her on a scholarship or a deferred-payment plan?" The filmmaker was moved by Bette's strong yet pitiful and compassionate appeal.

Bette Davis's genuine career began at that point. The Milton-Anderson school had the top teachers. She studied with George Arliss, a British and American stage and screen legend who came as a guest instructor and inspired his young charges with his interpretive abilities. He thereafter became an essential figure in her life. Davis was taught the ideas of complete bodily expression on stage by Martha Graham, another instructor. Graham, a disciplined, objective artist who would not lavish praise lightly, later remarked of her, "She had control, discipline, and electricity." I had a feeling she'd be something out of the ordinary." Bette shined in such roles as Mrs. Fair in The Famous Mrs. Fair, played on Broadway by then-popular performer Margalo Gillmore, during her two years there.

With her Milton-Anderson experience, she spent the next two years alternating between summer stock on the Cape and jobs in Rochester, New York, and elsewhere. Frank Conroy, who had maintained in touch with her, presented her to George Cukor, who was running a repertory company in Rochester in 1928. Given a small part on Broadway as a gum-chewing, tough chorus girl, she took over as the lead when the star was unavailable.

Davis proceeded to the Cape Playhouse in Dennis, Massachusetts, after receiving a promise from Cukor that she would be rehired as a resident ingenue in the fall. At first, she was only offered a job as an usher. She accepted and awaited her chance, unfazed. It came about when Laura Hope Crews, a well-known Broadway actress who was directing and playing the lead in a warhorse called Mr. Pim Passes By, sent out a request for a female who could assume an English accent. Davis overheard the request while dusting chairs and organising the evening's programs and exclaimed that she could fill the bill. Davis, who had mastered accents while at Milton-Anderson, obtained a commitment for the role—but only on the condition that she sing and play a certain ballad, I Passed by Your Window. Davis and Ruthie, who were unfamiliar with the tune, explored the music stores of adjacent towns until they located the sheet music. Davis played brilliantly and received plaudits, thanks to musician lover Ham's tuition in piano and singing at Cushing. Acting with Laura Hope Crews was a different story. Crews, who was too astute and professional not to perceive Bette's emerging talents, was particularly bothered by certain of her habits, particularly her proclivity to flap her arms around. The Great Lady became so enraged at one point that she struck Davis across the face. She also pushed her on another time. For the rest of the Cape run, her arms remained at her sides.

Davis was soon on her way back to Rochester, this time with her mother in tow, to complete her contract with the Cukor stock firm. It was the fall of 1928, and she was up against such stalwarts as Frank McHugh, Louis Calhern, Wallace Ford, and Elizabeth Patterson, all of whom went on to star in Hollywood films.

Miriam Hopkins was also present. Miriam was a seasoned Broadway leading lady at the age of twenty-six, imperious, demanding, temperamental, and a scene-stealer par excellence. Even back then, she'd honed her normal attention-getting techniques, such as fluttering handkerchiefs, picking up books, rubbing her throat, anything to divert focus away from a part player. Despite the fact that she had already had multiple husbands, lesbian rumours about her abounded; she fueled them by transporting a gorgeous young girl she called her "protégé," who withdrew with her into her bungalow straight after dinner, every night. Davis was perplexed when she patted her on the fanny and told her she had a gorgeous, swanlike neck. She invited Davis to join her and the girl in her bungalow one night, but Ruthie took her away on a pretext. "Stay away from her—she's trouble!" she exclaimed to Bette.

Miriam grew short with Bette after that when they played scenes together. Miriam yelled at Cukor one night, "She's stepping on my lines! The girl has no idea where she belongs! I'm the star of this show, not that insignificant nobody!" Davis, enraged and humiliated, drew her horns in by sheer force of will.

Years later, George Cukor denied firing Davis on the spot. "Her talent was obvious," he said. Yes, she did defy orders. She had her own opinions, and despite the fact that she only played bits and ingenue roles, she wasn't afraid to voice them. Her mother, as I recall, pushed her constantly and was always snooping around. However, I did not fire her. She insists I did, claiming I had a negative view of her at the time. But I deny everything!" Whatever the specifics of the incident were, she unexpectedly left the stock business. Davis was replaced after Louis Calhern, the experienced and seasoned character actor, complained in a piece called Yellow that she looked more like his daughter than his mistress. Calhern subsequently said that she was too aloof with the local Lotharios and refused to "put out," which made her unpopular.

2.

Struggling to the Surface

Davis's short stay in Rochester, on the other hand, proved to be the darkness before the day. The brilliant James Light cast her in Virgil Geddes' The Earth Between, which was staged at Light's Provincetown Playhouse in New York's Greenwich Village. That winter of 1929, Davis and Ruthie found a little flat on West Eighth Street and joyously and excitedly joined the famed group of bohemian artists of all stripes and persuasions, political, sexual, and cultural. "People can call their souls their own, and see who cares!" wrote one writer." To be sure, the MacDougal Street theatre was small, poorly heated, and filthy. It was, however, replete with memories of great actors and great plays, notably those of Eugene

O'Neill, and young Geddes, fresh from Nebraska, was as ecstatic about his brain-and-spirit-child being staged there as Davis was about acting in it. Washington Square was nearby, and across on Sixth Avenue and further in Sheridan Square, there were delightful little clubs and coffee cafes where current political and art movements were debating. Davis and Ruthie adored the Village environment, occasionally accompanied by Geddes or male cast members. She recalled "that wondrous sense of ecstatic freedom I knew while living there" many years later. There was an element of the unexpected and fantastic. I'm sorry for any artist of any stripe who hasn't experienced the life of Greenwich Village, however briefly or long."

Some have questioned whether Davis fully comprehended the plot of The Earth Between, or whether her Village-tour companion, the young dramatist Geddes, ever cared to inform her. Davis, who had developed a broad sensibility via voracious reading and persistent observation, must have been familiar with the phenomena of incest, at least in broad terms, by the age of twenty-one in 1929. And incest, however softly communicated, was the theme of The Earth Between. Davis must have recognized the play's underlying currents, for her performance as the frail, sensitive, delicate-spirited girl secluded on a Nebraska farm by her father's dominant personality received unanimous praise from a number of critics.

On the evening of March 5, 1929, many of her friends and neighbours gathered to cheer her on. Davis used all of her senses and emotions to bring the poor girl to life, armed with a run-of-the-mill contract for $35 per week (which sufficed far more amply than it would sixty years later). Before Breakfast, a brief Eugene O'Neill work, preceded the two-act play, but this was one night when O'Neill, who had helped make the Provincetown Players famous years before, took a back seat. It was her night. Davis responded with tremendous excitement to the applause and bravos of an informed and receptive audience, with Grover Burgess as her foreboding father and William Challee as her younger amorous vis-à-vis.

Nothing in her life, she subsequently said, could ever compare to the profound feelings and overwhelming elation she felt that night. New York had welcomed her with open arms. Her sole regret was that her father remained in Massachusetts; instead of attending the concert, he sent a bunch of flowers-complete with no note.

Bobby, Ruthie, and Uncle Paul Favor, a clergyman, all waited for the morning papers at the stand on West Eighth Street and Sixth Avenue. They delivered them to Davis, who burst into tears of ecstasy when the first reviews were read to her.

"Miss Davis," wrote Brooks Atkinson in The New York Times. ..St. John Ervine said in The New York World that she "is an entrancing creature who plays in a soft, unassertive style." According to the New York Daily News, "the performances are good, especially that of Miss Davis, a wraith of a child with true emotional insight."

The Earth Between played to packed houses and drew favourable press attention for Davis, who got a boost when legendary actress and producer Blanche Yurka wanted to visit her.

In 1929, Miss Yurka was a tremendous theatrical presence on the New York stage. Despite not being a particularly attractive or even attractive woman, she seized entire possession of the stage with captivating, flashing eyes, a dynamic, engaging chemistry, and a powerful theatrical air that commanded immediate attention. She had produced and starred in a number of outstanding classical and modern plays, as well as repertory, and was currently casting for the role of Hedvig in Ibsen's The Wild Duck. She'd gone to see Davis after reading the reviews, convinced she'd be perfect for the fragile, impassioned Hedvig, who commits herself after learning she's an unwanted child adopted by an uncaring father.

Miss Yurka didn't spend any time. When Davis and Ruthie arrived, she assured Davis that an audition was unnecessary and offered her the role of Hedvig. However, there was one tiny hurdle to overcome before Hedvig was hers. Davis awoke one morning with a severe case of measles. Fortunately, The Earth Between had finished its course, and Miss Yurka, determined that Davis play in The Wild Duck, postponed rehearsals for many weeks until she recovered.

Davis had caused problems during rehearsals and the run, according to Miss Yurka. "At first, she approached the role too enthusiastically. I wanted her to give it everything she had, which was a lot, but I had to temper and restrain her. Her apron-strings links to her mother, whom I thought was a stupid, flighty woman who had made her daughter her career, and in fact her entire existence, bothered me. She was the stereotypical stage mother-only worse. She was constantly present. She kept an eye on every male who came close to Bette, including her coworkers. I believe she believed that even a man's appearance might rape and/or impregnate!"

Miss Yurka, who was also in the play, responded to Davis's dedication by generously handing her entire scenes. "I've had my day; now let's see this eager, talented young lady have hers!"" She told the media. Davis received rave reviews when the play premiered in New York. "She acts with all her heart and being," said one critic. "On view here is a sincerity that is as compelling as it is electric."

Miss Yurka took the show on the road. Philadelphia's detractors were just as good. Davis was described as "strikingly effective" by a Philadelphian critic. .."[she] thrills us with the poignant grief that comes with the revelation of the child's great tragedy," The Washington Post opined, adding, "Bette Davis is a young woman who will advance far in her stage endeavours." She had been. ..Miss Yurka was taking Davis out to take curtain calls with her by this time; she treated Davis like a co-star, which Davis will be eternally grateful for. Davis would later describe Yurka, "People thought her formidable, frightening, and cold." I got to know the warm heart, admiration for good work, and ardent dedication to the acting craft that were at the centre of this amazing woman firsthand."

The Wild Duck's tour made its way to Boston-Boston, where she had fostered adolescent ambitions and hopes and felt the depths of sorrow when she feared nothing would ever happen, nothing would ever begin. The Boston Post gushed, "Our Miss Davis, practically our native daughter with her birth in Lowell and former residence in our suburbs, does us proud in one of Ibsen's finest, most demanding classic roles." She is heartbreaking and riveting as she shares her tremendous pain and loss."

Friends from Lowell, Lynn, Winchester, Newton, and Cushing Academy arrived. Harlow Morrell Davis finally emerged in the crowd, and subsequently in her dressing room. He remarked on the abilities of other cast members, the director, the play itself, and then went on to the weather, as usual unable to express what he was feeling (or probably not experiencing). He said nothing about her performance. Later, at home, he wrote her a formal, accurate message, the highlight of which, after perfunctory congratulations, was an order to eat healthily, because he believed she looked peaked.

During the tour, Davis also gained experience with another Ibsen play, The Lady From the Sea. Yurka thought this would be a fantastic contrast for her because she played a joyful, young, and carefree girl, exhibiting her ability to convey both youthful lightheartedness and expectation as well as devastating grief. Overall, the Yurka-Ibsen tour greatly broadened Davis's abilities and finally convinced her that she had a future in acting.

Davis returned to the Cape Playhouse for more seasoning after the tour concluded. With her days of ushering and bit-parting behind her, she spent the summer of 1929 honing her skills in a number of exciting positions. She remarked of her summer stock experiences,

"It keeps you on your toes; it teaches you timing, discipline, and control."

Marion Gering, who would later do some compelling early-thirties talkies, saw her in The Lady From the Sea in the spring of 1929 and asked her to try out for the ingenue role in Martin Flavin's Broken Dishes, which was to open on November 5, 1929, at Broadway's Ritz Theater. She would co-star in it alongside the funny yet touching actor Donald Meek, a fussy, bald-headed small man whose peculiarly androgynous, put-upon aura would eventually gain him enormous reputation as a character actor in Hollywood.

In Broken Dishes, Meek plays a milquetoast worm who, with the help of his feisty daughter, Davis, takes on his dictatorial battle-axe of a wife. Davis, who plays Elaine, the brave daughter, delivers a speech in Act III in which she scolds her mother and her friends in superb, stirring manner. The audience applauded her warmly at the curtain call, and, as Blanche Yurka had done, the gracious Mr. Meek, despite being the star, beckoned her out for curtain calls with him. Meek had lost his life's fortunes in the devastating Wall Street crash of October 1929, yet he came on and played his act with all his squirrelly sharpness that same night, according to Davis. "One of the most prime examples of the old saw about the show must go on that I was ever to witness," she subsequently said. It was a memory that sustained me in later years when I was too unwell to get out of bed but forced myself to travel to work where I knew the cast, crew, and director of a costly project that relied on my presence were waiting."

"Here is a young woman born for the theatre," a New York World reporter said of her performance in Broken Dishes. The plot of the play is small and maybe a little worn, but Miss Davis and Mr. Meek makes it seem fresh and new-and yes, even meaningful."

Broken Dishes was a huge success. Davis received fan mail from young ladies and men who saw themselves in her character and her family problems. It lasted for 178 performances until the spring of 1930, and Davis's name was prominently displayed in advertisements and on billboards. She was now a well-known Broadway personality, usually cited in gossip columns. Success was nice, even if she and Ruthie knew she still had a long way to go. They would occasionally take the subway from their East Fifty-third Street apartment to the Village to see the latest Provincetown show. Davis adored the Village and considered settling down in one of the historic nineteenth-century houses on Patchin Place. Ruthie and Bobby, on the other hand, felt she should stay as near to her Broadway theatre as possible.

A Samuel Goldwyn talent scout noticed her in Broken Dishes at this time and secured her her first screen test. The scout thought she could be appropriate for a role in Goldwyn's new Ronald Colman film, The Devil to Pay. Davis made the long trek to the Astoria studios in Queens several times due to scheduling delays and false-alarm photographic tests, but the test that eventually resulted convinced the Hollywood Powers-That-Be that Bette Davis had no future in cinema. "Her looks are too erratic. She's not glamorous or attractive enough. Goldwyn's scouts informed him, "She's a problem to light, and she doesn't have enough's.a.'" (1929 jargon for sex appeal). According to reports, he went to see her test himself and burst out screaming, "Who in hell did this to me? She's a canine!" Twelve years later, he would pay $385,000 to have that same "dog" loaned out for a film.

Davis, for her part, seemed unconcerned by the screen test findings. Her desire was to be a success on the stage, which she was, and she shared a sceptical, if not dismissive, attitude toward the West Coast movie studios with many of her colleagues. She brushed it off with no thought. She was even more pleased when her beloved "Madame," Grandmother Favour, the materfamilias, came to see her in Broken Dishes and called her granddaughter a signal success and a credit to the long line of Favors and Davises with uncharacteristic effusiveness.

Davis went on tour with Broken Dishes when it closed on Broadway, then returned to the Cape for her third season. Another tour of the successful Broken Dishes was planned for the fall, but when she was in Washington, she was requested to fill in as Alabama in The Solid South, starring the legendary old theatre luminary Richard Bennett. He was the father of Joan, Barbara, and Constance Davis would one day be likened to in Hollywood, a once-handsome guy who had gone to colourful seed through drink and dissipation but was still a stage personality to be reckoned with. His crazy improvisations and rude, furious asides thrilled spectators as much as his still-excellent acting did. Rouben Mamoulian, later the famed Hollywood director of Greta Garbo and Marlene Dietrich, directed, and his conflicts with old Bennett maintained the rehearsals in a perpetual state of commotion.

Bennett insisted on the approval of everyone he worked with, and when Davis arrived at rehearsal after a long journey from Washington, he yelled, "You're another of those young kids who think your eyes will do your acting for you, eh?"" Davis, tired from being on the train all night, drew herself up in twenty-two-year-old dudgeon and gave Bennett and the onlookers a preview of Mildred and Margo Channing by barking back, "I don't need this! Mr. Bennett, I can always return to Washington!"

Bennett, taken aback, then amused and fascinated, informed her she'd be good as Alabama. Bennett dominated the action as a flamboyant old colonel who commands his plantation and his children and drives everyone insane in The Solid South, a pretty tumultuous mix of farce and melodrama. Davis was the perfect loving and sensitive plantation belle as his daughter Alabama (a preview of her screen career). In the play, her light of love was attractive, sensitive Owen Davis, Jr., with whom she briefly "fell in crush," as she expressed it to Ruthie. He was the son of the dramatist who wrote Jezebel later in life.

Bennett, ever the cutup, would occasionally break character to demand a smoke "if I am to remain concentrating on this infernal pap!" One night, when the audience refused to respond to his comic sallies, he went to the footlights and barked, "I suppose I'll have to tell you stupid a nasty story to get you to laugh! You have no sense of taste! You're as foolish as they come! If you're not enjoying what you're witnessing, get up and leave!"

Bobby called Owen Davis, Jr. a "dreamboat" and teased Bette about him. "And consider this: if you married him, you wouldn't even have to change your name!"" She giggled, earning a swat from her sister. According to her acquaintances, the Owen Davis, Jr. encounter would have happened if he hadn't been romantically preoccupied elsewhere. He was the most recent of a dozen young guys she had met during her time in the theatre. One young man of excellent aristocratic pedigree provided her a rush for a time before pulling out by writing her a Dear John letter in which he indicated that his parents didn't approve of actors and that he couldn't see her anymore. Fortunately for her emotional health, Davis's focus in 1930 was primarily on her professional goals. And Ham was always there, a foreshadowing of things to come.

The Solid South closed after only thirty-one performances, possibly due to popular fatigue with Richard Bennett's untrustworthy pranks. Davis was called by Universal Pictures talent scout David Werner after regaining his freedom. He told her that the company was going to cast a film adaptation of Preston Sturges' Strictly Dishonorable, and she appeared perfect for the lead. She headed back across the river to Astoria to put her theory to the test. She took greater care with her grooming and makeup this time, and she barely passed the test. "They'll fix you up out there to look better," Werner said flatly as he handed her a contract for $300 a week with three-month options. "You're not the most sexy or glamorous girl I've sent out

West, but you've got intensity," he went on to say. "I think you'll go a long way in Hollywood."

3.

Hollywood

After a three-day train ride they described as "dusty, messy, and endless," Davis and Ruthie arrived in Hollywood on December 13, 1930. Bette told her mother as they stepped off the train that the thirteenth was not a good omen. Ruthie responded that a fortune teller had predicted that Bette Davis's name would one day be known all across the world, and that maybe-just maybe-movies would make that happen. After all, wasn't Charlie Chaplin a world-famous movie star? "I'm not a comedian, Ruthie," Davis said sarcastically.

Late 1930s Hollywood was still recovering from the Talkie Revolution of the previous year. Silence reigned supreme in 1927, the year Jolson's The Jazz Singer premiered. By 1929, the vast majority of motion movies were talking-or squawking-or squealing, depending on the quality of the sound recording in a given studio. Many a romantic star who had specialised in dynamic face-making backed by full orchestra had his or her voice revealed to be a Bronx honk or a less euphonious Southern drawl. Talkies were the end of great stars like Norma Talmadge and John Gilbert, though the latter was alleged to have been a victim of a sound-tampering conspiracy by his MGM boss Louis B. Mayer to cancel his pricey contract. But the scene was changing. In 1930, great silent stars like Mabel Normand and Lon Chaney died. Garbo had triumphed in Anna Christie, and her deep, intriguing Swedish inflections had enthralled viewers. An invasion of musicals had run its usefulness, and new talkie stars like Clark Gable were set to make their big screen debut.

The great studios, such as MGM, Paramount, and United Artists, were importing stage performers by the carload, and Ruth Chatterton, Clive Brook, Kay Francis, and other Broadway legends were negotiating lucrative contracts and an adoring screen audience. Warner Bros. had created a name for themselves with crime flicks.

Universal Pictures, along with RKO and Columbia, were among the second-rateers in late 1930, though all three would quickly rise to more renowned positions. Universal had created a splash with the superb All Quiet on the Western Front, based on the novel by Erich Maria Remarque. The new horror cycle, which included Frankenstein and Dracula, also benefited Universal's coffers that year and the following. Universal had huge ambitions for the future under elderly Carl Laemmle, one of the original film pioneers, and his young son, Carl Laemmle, Jr., and importing prominent theatre stars was part of their scheme.

But Davis was doomed from the outset. The man sent to meet her returned to the studio, stating that no one who resembled an actress had gotten off the train. Recognizing his error, he rushed back in time to accompany Bette and Ruthie to their hotel. The snapshot taken that day at the Plaza Hotel by the Universal camera aide conveys the narrative plainly enough: Davis appears nervous and tentative, her grin reluctant. Ruthie, dressed similarly to Bette in a generic cloche hat and a drab black coat, appears more determined but still sceptical.

Davis was drab and unappealing to Carl Laemmle, Jr., who preferred more glamorous, "obvious" instances of feminine attraction. He gave Strictly Dishonorable to Sidney Fox, a more obvious sexpot, and considered Davis for Walter Huston's A House Divided, "since we're stuck with her," but changed his mind. While waiting outside his office one day, Davis overheard him telling an aide, "That Davis dame has about as much appeal as Slim Summerville"-the ultimate humiliation, for Slim was an angular, unattractive, stupid-looking comedian whose stock in trade was his bewildered appearance and clumsy, shambling mannerisms. The ultimate attack, however, came from House Divided director William Wyler. "What do you think of these dames who show their chests and think they can get jobs!" Wyler chuckled."

She was then summoned to an office with no name or department heading on the door, where she was told flatly that the name "Bette Davis" sounded like a servant or a nurse, and that something more glamorous had been devised for her. "Bettina Dawes" was revealed as the inspiration. Davis, in a previously unseen flash of spirit, informed them that she refused to live her life with a name that sounded like Between the Drawers. Then she strode out with authority. When Junior Laemmle learned of her retort-and her attitude-he decided to let her keep her name. And the flicker of a hunch that there was more to her than her outward aspect reached him briefly, but quickly vanished, sadly for Davis.

They were at a loss for what to do with Bettina-Determined- to-Stay-Bette, so they sent her to the photo gallery to pose in various outfits-swimsuits, negligees, and street clothes. They were unimpressed by the images. Davis spent the last few weeks of 1930 reading Photoplay about Richard Bennett's stunning daughter Constance, who had advanced to a $30,000-a-week salary level and was the envy of every actress in Hollywood. Because the only screen actress Davis had ever taken seriously was Greta Garbo, whose screen image charmed her, she went with Ruthie to advance showing of Inspiration, the new Garbo picture, and then followed it to theatres. For hours, she studied Garbo's strange chemistry, her mannerisms, her facial expressions, and the strange, interesting way the camera made love to her.

They kept her busy on a couch while twenty men lay on top of her playing love scenes to test their on-camera "capabilities." They came and went, "like wooden soldiers," as she later told Ruthie, and only the courtly Gilbert Roland had the taste and tact to whisper to her, just before imposing his 170 pounds on her bosom, "It will be okay." Really! Everyone out here has to go through this at first."

The dictionary defines "lugubrious" as "exaggeratedly or affectedly mournful"—which is how The New York Times described Bette Davis's debut film performance in March 1931. Davis was slightly encouraged when she learned she would be appearing in a film adaptation of Booth Tarkington's The Flirt, but then she learned she would be playing the good sister, Laura, who is quiet, demure, virtuously predictable—and as dull as dishwater.

Strictly Dishonorable's British-born Sidney Fox got to play the lead character, who went through several name changes, including What a Flirt and Gambling Daughters, before Junior Laemmle opted on Bad Sister, reputedly to favour Fox, whom he was grooming for stardom. According to Davis, Junior and Sidney were having a heated romance, which explained all of her favouritism. Marianne, a daring, wicked, flirty, alluring woman sought after by the males of a little Indiana town, was to be played by Fox. Humphrey Bogart, who had only been in films for a year, played the mischievous con-man who seduces and then abandons Fox. Sadder and wiser, the one-time hey-hey girl marries staid solid-citizen Bert Roach, and dreary Laura wins the attractive doctor, Conrad Nagel, who learns his passion with Fox was a one-sided affair.

It's ironic that Davis's first role should feature her as an unrequited lover—at least until the happy ending—because unrequited love was to become one of her specialties. She swoons for the attractive Nagel, who wastes his sterling, upright feelings on the sluttish Fox for sixty-two of the sixty-eight minutes the picture runs.

Bogart was in her debut film and even had several sequences with her, but Davis loathed him from the outset and nothing changed her mind later in life, even when they did good work together. "How can you act so well with him if you dislike Bogie so much?""Louella Parsons once asked Davis, who responded sarcastically, "Because that's what I am-an actor!" If it's worth it to me, I'll work up a storm with Lucifer himself!"

Bogart was unmistakably playing Lucifer in Bad Sister. He first has Fox falsify her father's signature on an endorsement in order to collect funds to start a factory, then he flees with the dough and the daughter-and subsequently abandons her. Raymond Schrock and Tom Reed kept some of the Tarkington flavour, with additional language by Edwin Knopf. Karl Freund, known for his silent-era German masterpieces, found himself befuddled by the immobile cameras, noisy traffic incursions, and odd microphone placements in 1931 Hollywood. Freund placed a small microphone between Davis's breasts, forcing her to restrict her head motions; she spent the most of the time talking directly into her mammaries.

Conrad Nagel, who played her love interest, had a successful silent film career and assisted Louis B. Mayer in establishing the Academy of Motion Picture Arts and Sciences while teaching Mayer on a more "cultured" accent. Nagel had a wonderful voice for talkies, but Mayer overlooked him in the early talkie era, and his acting career sank progressively. Hedda Hopper reportedly said of the MGM tycoon, "It's bad luck to help Louie Mayer-he never forgets to repay favours with unkindness," and Nagel proved this to be all too true. However, Adela Rogers St. Johns felt that Nagel had offended Mayer by telling one too many people how hard he had worked to "refine L. "I'm trying to change B.'s accent into something more civilised."

Conrad Nagel spoke with me about Davis and her debut picture in 1960.

"She was quite bashful and insecure. I believe she understood she wasn't wanted by the powers that be, which naturally damaged her confidence. She was, as I subsequently discovered, entirely inexperienced with sex and very embarrassed. A twenty-three- year-old virgin in a rather unvirginal Hollywood! That was unprecedented in 1991!" Nagel chuckled.

When asked why Davis disliked Bogart so much, he recalled that in one scene with him, Davis had to diaper a baby; she had expected it to be a girl; when she discovered she had to handle a boy's genitals, doubtless the first male genitals she had ever seen, and she was only twenty-three!-as Davis recalls, she blushed a deep scarlet throughout the scene, which appeared grey on screen. Nagel suspected Bogart was cheating on her virginity and had gathered cast and crew to observe her response. He appeared to think it was all a great joke. Bogart could also be vulgar. "That dame is too uptight; what she needs is a good screw from a man who knows how to do it," that's what he said to Nagel.

"She didn't understand anything about makeup or eyelining or rouging or the right kind of lipstick for the camera, and nobody went out of their way to enlighten her," he said. "She had to stand by and watch all those prissy makeup men buzzing around court favourite Sidney Fox making her look divine; Marie Antoinette must have felt the same way about DuBarry in her early days!'"

Sidney Fox, who knew Davis's clout in the front office and, in his perspective, liked making Davis look drab and unwelcome, also pulled rank, according to Nagel. "Her hair was ash-blonde at the time, and it photographed a mousy brown." "She told me later that she and her mother left the San Bernardino preview before it was over, because she felt that humiliated, absolutely hated herself on the screen; did for years in fact." Even Variety's kind reference to her ("Bette Davis holds much promise in her handling of Laura, sweet, simple, and the very essence of repression") did little to console her. Only Karl Freund saw her potential: "She has lovely eyes," he told Junior Laemmle, despite the fact that the Times had dubbed her "lugubrious." That remark apparently rescued her at Universal—at least for a while.

John M. Stahl, a filmmaker recognized as one of the screen's arch sentimentalists, was ready to begin work on Seed, a film based on Charles G. Norris' controversial novel about birth control. Because the birth control theme was too strong for the wary Hays Office, Gladys Lehman's screenplay evolved into a banal, somewhat tedious story about a man, John Boles, who wants to be a writer but is suffocated by the demands of family life, which includes five children and a wife, Lois Wilson, who is too sweet and self-sacrificing for words. He eventually abandons his family, becomes a famous novelist, takes on slender, smooth Genevieve Tobin as a mistress-and then begins to wonder about the people he abandoned, including his now-grown children.

Stahl had no trouble playing the four sons, but the daughter, Margaret, was a stickler. She had to be wraithlike, vulnerable, charming and energetic all at the same time. He scoured high schools, drama forums, theatres, restaurants, and wherever else save the Universal contract list until spotting Davis in the Universal commissary and deciding she was the appropriate fit. The monumentally unimpressed Laemmles, who was utterly unimpressed with Davis's Bad Sister antics, immediately agreed to Stahl or anybody else keeping Davis busy while she worked out her contract option, and Davis arrived in Seed, where she was scarcely seen or heard by audiences. "If you blinked, you missed her, the role was that small," one of her "brothers," Raymond Hackett, later recalled to his wife, Blanche Sweet, who told me:

"Raymond said she was the most pathetic thing he had ever seen—unsure of herself, thoroughly aware she was unappreciated, disregarded by everyone, especially Stahl." After pushing her into the background, the director promptly forgot about her, and Davis practically directed herself through the few scenes she had in Seed.

"There was no makeup man for me, no attempt was made to light me properly, and I felt like a churchmouse next to the soignée Genevieve Tobin, who broke up our dull but happy home," she later remembered, bitterly. ..But I did my onerous duty and remained silent. ...If I wasn't already dead in photos, this appearance was sure to do the trick." She also recounted feeling like a "ghost" in the presence of Tobin, Lois Wilson, Hackett, and Richard Tucker.

Hackett confided in his wife, Blanche Sweet, that he was certain Davis had formed a woman-size crush on gorgeous John Boles, the star at the time, who was thirty-seven years her senior. Mr. Boles had been in films for roughly seven years, alternating between singing leads and love foils for actresses such as Gloria Swanson and Bebe Daniels. Gentlemanly and soft-spoken, with the breeding of a southern aristocrat, Mr. Boles had lit a mighty fire in the heart of the young Norma Shearer, among others, and was to prove the ultimate homme fatal of cinema opposite Irene Dunne, whom he heartlessly relegated to the Back Street, and Ann Harding, whose heart he broke in a somewhat similar fashion in The Life of Vergie Winters. But, sadly for Davis, Boles was no philanderer or taker when it came to exploiting the vulnerabilities of his young coworkers.

When the film was released in May 1931, Universal thought so little of her that she wasn't even featured in the advertising, and her name was way down on the list of credits. When I saw Seed in revival a few years ago, I thought Davis was bland, dull, and ZaSu-Pitts-like. (In fact, ZaSu appeared in the film as a maid, and Davis appeared to be impersonating the limp-wristed, fluttery comedian.) The film itself seemed to lack the courage of its convictions, having been boiled down from a novel with more bite and bark, and the plot meandered uneasily. "Lethargic and often dull," according to The New York Times.

Davis had been someone's sister for the third time. Reviewers ignored her again in Waterloo Bridge, a cinematic adaptation of

Robert E. Sherwood's play, as she faded away in a poorly written, ill-defined role as the hero's sister who is courteous to the tiny showgirl with whom he falls in love before departing for the World War I front from England. The showgirl-turned-prostitute dies on Waterloo Bridge, believing she has squandered her decency as well as the right to her lover's esteem and consideration.

Such are the bare bones of this terrible drama, which was done twice more, first in a considerably superior MGM version starring Vivien Leigh and Robert Taylor in 1940, and once in a forgettable 1956 attempt starring Leslie Caron and John Kerr, retitled Gaby for no apparent reason.

The 1931 version was certainly a slapdash, ramshackle affair, devoid of proper movie underscoring and hampered by superficial performances from the leads, Mae Clarke (more famous for getting Cagney's grapefruit jammed in her face in The Public Enemy) and Kent Douglass, who later, as Douglass Montgomery, would sparkle briefly in films opposite Katharine Hepburn and Margaret Sullavan.

During the shoot, Douglass developed feelings for Davis, but she deemed him too frail and effeminate for her tastes (Margaret Sullavan later expressed similar reservations about him), and as his growing interest did little for her ego, she quickly discouraged it.

Davis recalled hovering about the set, mouthing Mae Clarke's lines and wishing she could perform the role the way she thought it should be done. Eager, sad, frustrated, and disappointed, she was as much a wraith on set as she was in front of the camera, as coworkers recall, and she was once again forgotten, both in the commercials and in the reviews. "Janet was an insipid part," she grumbled later. "I think I had four lines in it, and I don't think I changed my costume." I was meant to be pleasant to Clarke, but I secretly despised her since she was getting the spotlight I knew I could have done credit to!"

Mae Clarke was an actor with obvious limitations, and she wasn't particularly attractive. Later in her career, she was forced to play little parts as a feminine counterpart for Cagney and others. When I interviewed her many years later, she commented, "Gosh, in 1931 I felt I was really on my way, and Bette seemed to be in permanent Loser-Limbo." I don't recognize her from the photo. She appeared to be trying hard not to draw attention to herself. It's hard to believe that this bashful stick of a girl would flame up the screen in sizzling, sexual roles within a year or two. Of course, her hair was a brownish ash-blonde at the time, and it wasn't really appealing. She also lacked fashion sense, something the studio did not help her with. But it must have taken a strong determination to break out from the rut she was in when I knew her-certainly she demonstrated it in spades."

Years later, Davis allegedly sought to get down-and-out Make a small part in one of her major Warner starrers from the 1940s. Davis stated, "I was a nothing also-ran in her picture, and maybe I can help her do just a little more in mine now." However, those who knew Davis well at the time felt that she was attempting to reestablish a contrast-in petty reverse-with an actress whom she had bitterly envied, given her frustrating 1931 situation at Universal. In this case, her intentions were most likely mixed.

Waterloo Bridge was mostly met with chilly, perfunctory dismissal by the critics. "There are moments when the story has a sympathetic tug," Variety sneered, slamming with tepid praise.

Davis was first disappointed to find that she would be loaned out to RKO for Other People's Business, later retitled Way Back Home. Mr. and Mrs. Phillips Lord, who had earned considerable popularity in a regular NBC radio show called Seth Parker, where to feature in it. Mr. Lord, a folksy, do-gooder Maine pastor, answered his people's issues, consoled them in their distress, and was a positive and uplifting influence.

Based on the radio personalities, Jane Murfin wrote a warm, homey, unaffected screenplay. The plot, what there was of it, revolved around wicked Stanley Fields (one of the film's favourite heavies of the time) attempting to wrest unfortunate son Frankie Darro away from the Lords, with whom he had sought safety. Throughout the novel, Fields clashes with not just the Lords, but also with local youngster Frank Albertson and his girl, Davis, who befriends Darro. Fields is eventually killed by a train, and everything ends sweetly.

The film had a $400,000 budget (a lot for the time) and ran for an unusually long 81 minutes. It was full of warm, informal, unassuming Maine touches, and the village life and people are caught without Hollywoodish elaborations and came through as authentic and human.

Davis was not only pleasantly delighted at the cordial and gracious treatment she received at RKO from Producer Pandro Berman, who had been captivated by her promise in her Universal movies and had asked for her, but to her delight realised, by glancing at the rushes, that photographer J. Roy Hunt had exposed her to greatest advantage, showcasing her excellent eyes and expressive mouth. Director William Keighley, who excelled at light and sentimental romance, understood actresses (he married two of them, Laura La Plante and Marian Nixon) and took time and care with her scenes. While she was merely a supporting player as Frank Albertson's girlfriend, she appeared in Way Back Home to far greater advantage than she had in any previous film.

Soon she had attracted the notice of the screen's leading magazine editor, James R. Quirk of Photoplay, who kept his Hollywood staff moving on Davis. One of his writers, Katherine Albert, recalled to me her visit to the RKO set in late 1931, where she found Davis relaxing contentedly with an orangeade in the company of Frank Albertson, who was obviously smitten with her. Now Davis was reading about herself in Photoplay.

"She was a shy little thing-almost mousey-in those days," Katherine told me in 1953. "It is amazing, in retrospect, why I didn't sense the fire in her at that time. Maybe it was the part she was playing-a nice, small-town Maine girl-and she was living it on and off screen. She spoke of her love for her mother and sister, and her hopes for the future. I had heard she was very unhappy with the treatment she was getting at Universal, but she seemed hesitant to go into detail about it, at least on that occasion. I guess she didn't want to seem to bite the hands that fed her-though actually they were starving her, both creatively and monetarily. A month or so later, after they let her go, she told me, 'They said I had no sex appeal, and they couldn't imagine any man giving me a tumble. I was regarded as attractive back in New York, and I had plenty of beaux; in fact, turned down several proposals of marriage. If they had paid more attention to me, if they had photographed and directed me differently, and had given me parts I could have shown my mettle in, they might have felt respect for me. But that is all water under the bridge now, thank goodness.'"

Director William Seiter said of her in 1960: "I found her a cooperative and delightful actress, and the Lords were like parents to her, concerned and hospitable. Universal had handled her very stupidly, of course-they didn't realise what they had in her, and it didn't say much for their perspicacity. She claimed that Way Back Home was the first film in which she felt she had been properly showcased, and that it gave her hope for the future. Everyone liked her, and she worked hard with what slight material she was given. She was graphically agitated, I remember, in a scene where Stanley Fields, the drunken father of Darro, is menacing her, and her love scenes with Frank Albertson were tender. Frank was obviously in love with her, and she handled him very gently, onscreen and off."

Frank Albertson, who began as a prop boy in movies at thirteen in 1922, was twenty-two when he made Way Back Home. In 1960, he was in New York on vacation when Psycho, in which he had a small part, premiered, and reminisced about his career in general. He had played many leads and such outstanding character parts as Katharine Hepburn's brother Walter in Alice Adams, in which he had really shone with critics and public. While his career in 1960 was on a decided downslide, he was mellow and philosophical while we talked.

He said he had most enjoyed acting with Katharine Hepburn, among the many stars he had supported, but reserved some affectionate words for Bette Davis and Way Back Home.

"It was a really warm and homey little picture. The Lords, whom I felt I already knew from their radio program, created a family atmosphere on the set, and yes, I did develop a crush on Bette. She was very warm and sweet. I know people think of her as fussy, man-hating, dynamo and temperamental but she wasn't like that then, not at all. I really felt the love scenes but I could tell her romantic interests were elsewhere; I believe she married Harmon Nelson some months later. But we were always friendly when we met in later years."

Davis always defended Way Back Home as a warm, genuine film, but the January 1932 critical opinion was mixed. "Unbelievably bad," sniffed Weekly Variety but The New York Times called it "real and mellow."

After Way Back Home finished filming, Universal kicked Davis over to yet another studio, Columbia, for The Menace. In later years Davis said of The Menace (the original title had been The Feathered Serpent), "It was a monstrosity; my part consisted of a great many falls out of closets. The picture was made in eight days. I knew I had obviously reached bottom."

The director, Roy William Neill, accorded the hapless Davis scant attention, and the love interest to whom she was assigned, Walter Byron, drank heavily, smoked incessantly, and though only thirty, was obviously on the downgrade, which accounted for his strangely aged and bloated appearance. He also had the foulest breath of any man she had ever met, and this made the love scenes with him a particular trial for Davis.

After several heavy woo-pitching scenes, Davis couldn't stand it anymore and asked Byron, "Do you ever brush your teeth or use mouthwash? You show a shocking lack of consideration for me when you forget about such things!" Roy William Neill told a Photoplay writer ten years later that "when she lit into Byron like that, I knew there was more-much more-to her. It's no wonder to me that by now [1942] that little girl has battled her way to the top like a champ!"

Natalie Moorhead, a well-groomed and handsome blonde actress also in the picture, was some years Davis's senior and was obviously jealous and insecure in her scenes with the visitor from Universal and tried to upstage her. Her tactics-moving upstage away from the camera, forcing Davis to turn around and face her, and so on, prepared Davis for combat with another egotistical star, Miriam Hopkins, some years later. "Natalie was a cold egotist," H. B. Warner, also in the cast, said. "She was very self-conscious and self-protective about her looks and general appearance and I am afraid she gave the little Davis girl a hard time."

The plot was some trivial nonsense about Byron fleeing England after being falsely accused of murdering his father. He is disfigured in the oil fields of the southwest United States, returns to England to learn who killed his father, and finally pins the murder on his stepmother, Moorhead, and her cohort. Disguised by the plastic surgery that his accident had necessitated, he pretends to be a prospective buyer for the ancestral estate, fooling both his stepmother and his former fiancée, Peggy, played by Davis. Davis and he are reunited at the unconvincing fadeout.

Byron, who had made a glittering start as Gloria Swanson's leading man in Queen Kelly in 1928, told an at first sympathetic but finally bored and irritated Davis during on-set tea sessions that he felt he was all through in America and perhaps should return to his native England. "You're full of self-pity and that is destructive," she told him. "Stop the drinking and smoking and watch your health and looks, and maybe things will get better." She always expressed regret in later years that this very handsome man and good actor obviously hadn't taken her advice. Byron took a small part in what turned out to be his last film in 1939, and then lived on in total obscurity until 1972.

The Menace was a hopelessly bad film in all departments, from Roy William Neill's perfunctory get-it-over-and-done-with style of direction to the careless photography, which did nothing for Davis, to the screenplay by Dorothy Howell and Charles Logue, which never got off the ground.

Some of the photographs the still department dreamed up were the silliest and most inappropriate possible. One that is often reprinted shows Byron and Davis staring up at an obviously pâpier-maché "monster." They were so poorly posed by the photographer that they didn't even look frightened-just bored. As well they might have been. The reviews of the time shrugged it off with "just routine melodrama without menace or perceptible suspense." Weekly Variety, though, delighted a certain someone with, "Bette Davis has to take a decided second to Natalie Moorhead." Another sniffed: "Filled with absurd situations." When I saw it many years later, I felt the original reviewers had been too kind.

Hell's House, shot in 1931 and released in early 1932, was certainly the nadir of Davis's early Hollywood career. "It took two weeks to shoot and looked like it had taken a day and a half," the witty Irish-

American actor Pat O'Brien later said of it. It was his first picture with Davis, and they became, in his words, "a mutual consolation society of two." Later Davis and her mother became excellent friends with Pat and his wife.

Davis once said of O'Brien, with whom she would work again, "He was very vital and sexy looking and acting and, I thought, a handsome man in his Irish-looking way, but playing around was not his thing. I don't know if it was Catholic guilt or what, but Pat always went home to the little wife; no womaniser was he." When kidded by his friends about his fidelity to his marriage vows, Pat always gave an unprintable rejoinder along the lines of Paul Newman's remark decades later about the reason for his fidelity to wife Joanne Woodward: "Why should I go out looking for quick hamburgers when I have steak at home?" Frank McHugh later said, "Pat could talk dirty with the best of us, but the funny thing was he never put his cock where his mouth was"-meaning action never followed the words.

Davis needed all the reassurance she could find in co-star O'Brien's friendship, for Hell's House, originally known as Juvenile Court, was a real horror. The last of the quickie films for which she had been haplessly shunted around by the Laemmles, it displayed her as Peggy, the girlfriend of flashy bootlegger Matt (O'Brien), who takes advantage of hero-worshipping teenager Jimmy (Junior Durkin) by letting him take the rap for one of his own offences. Junior winds up in reform school (Hell's House, of course), where the goings-on are as Dickensian as poverty-row producer Ben Zeidman and fly-by-night director Howard Higgin could make them. At the horror-pit, Jimmy befriends frail Shorty, (played by another young actor named Junior—in this case Junior Coghlan) who is dying, in properly bathetic style, of a heart ailment. A crusading newspaper publisher, Morgan Wallace, exposes conditions at the reform school, and all turns out well when the cowardly O'Brien, egged on by indignant girlfriend Davis, finally acts like a man and accepts the responsibility for the crime he had foisted on the innocent Junior Durkin.

Junior Durkin was sixteen when he made Hell's House. A promising young juvenile with a sensitive face and manner, he had been a hit in Huckleberry Finn earlier in the year, but after that found himself a "has-been," and made only a few films after Hell's House before his death at twenty in a car crash of which his good pal, the famed child star Jackie Coogan, was the only survivor.

"Junior was an unlucky kid," Pat O'Brien later said of him. "He was too boyish and innocent to graduate into leading-man status, and of course that early death was tragic. But he was so down, so disappointed over failing to make it when he loved acting so that maybe death came as a mercy, terrible and sad as that sounds."

O'Brien remembers young Durkin developed a tremendous adolescent crush on Davis, who, on and off the screen, adopted a big-sisterly, protective attitude toward him. "I think Junior, who could be very winsome and sweet, was the brother she had always wished she had," O'Brien remembered. "She and her mother went out of their way to be nice to him, and I think it came as a real shock to her when I tipped her off that the poor kid, all of sixteen, no less, had fallen hook, line, and sinker for her!"

While the picture was shot on peanuts in less than two weeks, producer Zeidman and director Higgin found it necessary to cut one scene in which Davis puts her arms around Junior to comfort him. "And they hated to cut it," Pat O'Brien later laughed, "because even two minutes of film loomed large in their budget, but for Christ's sake, the kid had a hard-on in his pants when Bette hugged and kissed him, and the camera caught it!"

Junior Coghlan and some of his pals, according to O'Brien, rescued the few feet of film from the cutting room wastebasket and for some years enjoyed showing it at their stag parties. "It so embarrassed Junior Durkin," according to O'Brien, "that he got into some fist fights trying to recover it. He came to me about a year later over it. 'What do I do?' he wailed. 'Laugh about it, and go around congratulating yourself. So you got a hard-on with Bette Davis in a movie-great-proves you're a man!'"

O'Brien couldn't resist passing the news about her young co-star's "humiliation" on to Davis, who found it amusing, in a self-deprecatory way. "Hell," O'Brien remembered her saying, "it isn't as if I were Jean Harlow or Connie Bennett or Lombard. Why, I was still a virgin then! If I got the poor kid excited, I guess I have to take it as a compliment. But I hadn't even dyed my hair a provocative blond at that time-I can't imagine what he saw in me!"

O'Brien laughed that a lot of adult males later would have commended adolescent Junior Durkin's taste circa 1931. "They were calling her a drab, sexless wren over at Universal, couldn't wait to get rid of her," O'Brien chortled, "but that horny kid saw what nobody else saw-no flies on him!"

Hell's House languished on the second- and third-bill poverty-row circuits but, unaccountably, got a New York release in early 1932. New York Times critic Mordaunt Hall wrote: "The direction of the film is old-fashioned. Pat O'Brien gives a forced performance. Young Durkin's playing is sincere and likewise that of Bette Davis." Weekly Variety dismissed the proceedings thus: "It merits only the attention of the second runs-the lesser ones. ...[It] projects as having been put together in a slipshod manner." O'Brien's summation of Hell's House was: "The only thing solid about it was Junior's hard-on-and that was cut!" Back at Universal they had news for Davis. With her latest option expired, she was let go.

4.

Warner, Zanuck-and Arliss

The end of her thankless Universal and loanout year was to herald the start of a brilliant new career at Warners, that most vital and energetic of companies.

In the new year of 1932, she would meet three men who would drastically alter the course of her career.

The first, Jack L. Warner, was one of four brothers of Polish-Jewish heritage who had moved to New York from Canada. Jack struggled up the cinema industry with his brothers, Harry, Albert, and Sam, from the nickelodeons he ran around 1910 to the short films he began creating in 1912. Warner Bros. released their first profitable film, My Four Years in Germany, in 1917, and by 1925, they had merged with First National Pictures and Vitagraph. They changed the industry in 1927 with the first film that merged songs with lines of conversation, The Jazz Singer, starring Al Jolson, after experimenting with sound in the John Barrymore film Don Juan in 1926. This propelled them to the forefront of cinema production, ushering in the Talkie Era. Harry became president of Warner Brothers in the early 1930s, Albert became treasurer, and Jack became director of production at the Burbank Studios in Hollywood (Sam had died in 1927).

Jack was a strong, bluff man who ruled his studio with an iron fist. He kept the timelines tight and the pay modest, and his assistants produced lean, quick, unadorned films that usually ran just over an hour. Darryl Zanuck (and later Hal Wallis) helped him put Warners on the map in the 1930-1933 period with a succession of gangster films and crisp social dramas that appealed to a Depression-era audience. Even the musicals that Warners became known for had a sharp, harsh edge, with striving chorus girls and male entertainers vying for the big break.

Jack Warner regarded his actors as his children and governed over them like a tyrannical, disciplined, but fair parent. Like the other greats of his generation—Mayer, Thalberg, Laemmle, Cohn, and Zukor—he developed personalities via consistent exposure, and the multiplicity of poor films he pushed on them was offset by the fact that he made many of them household names. Jack was known for his raffish, unsubtle sense of humour-it is said that when he was introduced to Madame Chiang Kai-shek, he made a joke about having forgotten to bring his laundry-but he also had a keen, instinctual taste for prestige values when he believed the time was right. He was to admire the talents of the illustrious George Arliss, as well as those of Paul Muni and Edward G. Robinson, among others.

Darryl Zanuck, his outstanding production assistant in 1932, contributed fully to the lurid but well-crafted gangster melodramas that made Cagney and Robinson stars, as well as the social consciousness and musical flicks. All were fast-paced, hard-edged, snappily structured, and lightly budgeted, but with Zanuck, less was more, and the outcome was effortlessly professional, devoid of excessive production values (save in the musicals).

Zanuck, who was born in Nebraska in 1902, participated in World War I before falling into writing following a succession of odd occupations. After working as a screenwriter for Warners since the age of twenty-one, he was promoted to studio manager in 1928 after successfully merchandising Rin-Tin-Tin films, and to production head in 1929. He gave Warners a terrific charge with his creative vigour. He was restless, innovative, and oversexed (his specialty was showing his heavy endowment to various lovelies on the lot). He left in 1933 to found Twentieth Century and ultimately to head over Twentieth Century-Fox, but when he and Davis met in 1932, he was the Warner lot's Big Gun (figuratively and literally).

Murray Kinnell, a renowned Broadway character actor who had played with Davis in The Menace, was impressed by her potential and recommended her to his friend George Arliss, who was working on a film at Warners called The Man Who Played God.

George Arliss was the leading character actor in cinema at the time (late 1931). In his sixties, he was a thin guy with a skeletal face and piercing eyes, far from attractive or even distinguished-looking, and he was not the sort that Hollywood and American moviegoers would take to their hearts. He made his stage debut in 1886, when he was eighteen years old. Then, on a tour in 1902, he arrived in the United States and reigned on Broadway for decades, eventually going into silent films and later talkies, where his distinct voice and style earned him an Oscar for Disraeli (1929-1930). In sophisticated, literate pictures like Old English, Alexander Hamilton, and The Green Goddess, his reputation grew. When Davis met him, he was Warners' most valuable and prestigious star.

Davis was about to leave Hollywood, had even purchased her plane tickets and was packed with her mother for the return trip to New York, when Arliss called and requested to see her. He was immediately taken with her appearance and demeanour, and based on his own trained intuition as well as Kinnell's recommendation, he cast her in the role of Grace, a young girl who is in love with his character, Montgomery Royale, a famous pianist who was deafened by a bomb meant for a king who was in attendance at one of his Paris concerts.

Back in America, terribly depressed by the prospect of never hearing again, Royale has taken a philanthropic interest in strangers he observes through his binoculars in Central Park, learning their difficulties by reading their lips and becoming their anonymous benefactor in a number of situations. When he later sees Davis in the park telling the young man she loves that she feels obligated to stay with Royale, whom she reveres and adores but is not physically in love with, he breaks off their engagement and marries Violet Heming, an older woman who has patiently waited for him.

Julian Josephson and Maude Howell wrote the screenplay, which was adapted from a short tale by Gouverneur Morris and the play The Silent Voice by Jules Eckert Goodman, and it was directed by John Adolfi in a rather pompous, old-fashioned manner that makes the film feel obsolete and falsely sentimental today. While the other performers are fine, and Arliss is his usual expert, captivating self, Davis is the film's revelation with her true, honest, and vivacious performance.

Arliss asked her how long she had been on stage during the interview. He replied to her three-year answer, "Just long enough to rub off the rough edges." He regarded her vivacious and engaging, but it wasn't until they were on a Warners sound stage for their first scene together that the full effect of her immense potential hit him.

I quoted the effect she had on Arliss in his second autobiography, My Ten Years in the Studios (1940), in a Bette Davis career study I published for Films In Review in 1955.

"I think only two or three times in my experience have I ever gotten something from an actor during rehearsal that was beyond what I realised was in the part." Bette Davis was one of those outliers. I knew she was playing a 'lovely small part' that was essential to me, so I prayed for the best. But when we rehearsed, she surprised me; the pleasant small part transformed into a deep and vivid creation, and I felt somewhat humiliated that this young girl [Davis was then twenty-three] had discovered and portrayed something that my mind had failed to imagine. She surprised me because I received a spark from her that lighted plain words and inspired them with passion and emotion. That is the kind of brightness that cannot be hidden, and I am not astonished that Bette Davis is now the most important star on the screen [1940]."

Davis not only wowed Arliss with her talent, but also with her dedication and professionalism. She wasn't some stupid ingenue passing the time, primping for the cameras in the hopes of arousing the romantic sensibilities of her male audience and eliciting feminine envy. She was already a maturely dedicated artist at the age of twenty-three, resolved to give her all at all times. She saw herself in the company of seasoned artists such as Violet Heming, Louise Closser Hale, and Ivan Simpson. She recognized that cameraman James Van Trees and director Adolfi were aiming for a "class" effect in all sectors, and she was determined to be a class act herself in this class setting.

Davis has always considered The Man Who Played God to be a watershed moment in her career. "The Man Who Played God was probably my most important picture," she stated. I did other things that I enjoyed better and were more substantial, but appearing as Mr. Arliss' leading lady gave me credibility."

She didn't know two things about Arliss at the moment. One was that he had requested entirely private screenings of every film she had worked on since arriving in Hollywood. He sighed at her neglect, at the lack of attention, at how the bushels of mediocrity had obscured her remarkable radiance. The other was that he had developed an immediate personal attraction to her, which he would never reveal to her. Arliss fell in love with Davis despite being 64 years old at the time. His patient and understanding wife of many years, Florence, who participated in several of his films, usually as his husband and supportive sidekick, had long tolerated his unapologetic ladies' man. Arliss's attention wandered right up until the gates of old age, but Florence kept his eternal affection and fidelity. When her eyesight worsened in 1937, he resigned from the screen forever to give her his complete care. Leslie Arliss, their son, went on to become a talented and accomplished director.

When Arliss performs the scene in which he lip-reads Davis's frustration over her unfulfilled love for attractive young Donald Cook and her desire to stand by a man who is forty years her senior, he does so with complete conviction. As events unfolded, he went on to make the same personal sacrifice offscreen.

Between takes, Arliss and Davis had long chats on the set, and he frequently brought her his favourite tea and scones. Davis noted how he made her feel like a true woman, a talented individual worthy of her peers' respect. The mood on the set of The Man Who Played God was so different from the casual, knockabout, helter skelter set environment at Universal that she became engrossed in its awe.

Arliss suggested she lighten her hair to a more vibrant shade of blond to make her appearance reflect her personality. It was sound counsel. After wardrobe provided her with a set of carefully fitted dresses and gowns that gave her a truly glamorous aspect onscreen for the first time, she consulted with Perc Westmore, Warners' makeup genius, who saw to it that her hair was carefully bleached, a chic, slickly conceived new hairdo was designed for her, and her makeup played up her assets and de-emphasized her liabilities.

"According to the standards of the world I came from [Broadway], I was a blonde—technically, an ash blonde," Davis said years later. My hair was unremarkable by 1930s Hollywood standards, when brilliant, bleached hair reigned supreme. [Perc] was astute enough to recognize [as Arliss did] that the blonder hair would enhance my photographic image. He was correct. For the first time, I looked like myself in The Man Who Played God. It was a new lease on life for me. In fact, I've been likened to Constance Bennett. I was extremely flattered. I'd always enjoyed how she seemed on the television."

The purported likeness to Connie Bennett would prove to be a mixed benefit for her during the next year. But, as she quickly realised, it all added up to good exposure.

Jimmy Van Trees' skillfully applied makeup and precise lighting (often recommended by Arliss himself, who understood angles better than anyone) completed the effect the New Bette Davis created in The Man Who Played God.

Weekly Variety was one of the periodicals to notice the New Bette, with its reviewer gushing: "A splendid production." ...The ingenue, Bette Davis, is a vision of wide-eyed blonde beauty."

George Arliss would reemerge in Bette Davis' life on a number of subsequent occasions. She had always admired him, and when he died in 1946, at the age of 78, she commented, "I owe Mr. Arliss more than I could ever repay." He was like a parent to me in a critical, important manner, the first major fosterer of my artistic life. Furthermore, his death is not only my loss; it is the loss of the entire planet."

Jack Warner signed Davis to a five-year contract with one-year options after viewing rushes of her performance in The Man Who Played God, apparently at the request of George Arliss himself. He hustled her into two new pictures at the same time, keeping her occupied as she moved from one set to the other. Both parts were supporting roles in films starring prominent stars, but she had strong material to work with and managed to shine despite little screen time.

So Big, an Edna Ferber novel, has already been filmed with Colleen Moore in 1925. Barbara Stanwyck, whose contract Warners shared with Columbia under a new agreement, was now playing Selina Peake, one of the daring ladies Ferber admired. Selina is a schoolteacher in the farming country of the West, and she has placed her hopes in her son, Hardie Albright, whom she wants to see become a renowned architect. He has other plans, such as womanising and stockbroking, but Selina will be pleased to know that she influenced her friend's son, George Brent, to become a famous sculptor. Dallas O'Mara, a young artist in love with Albright, is played by Davis. She realises and appreciates this plain woman's essential grandeur of spirit as she gets to know her, and Selina is left hoping that Dallas may influence her son to nobler endeavours.

Despite its briefness, Davis excelled in the role of Dallas. In later years, she stated that Dallas epitomised the assertive womanliness that she admired in herself. Her affinity with the idealistic yet practical Dallas was likely one of her self-delusions, since Dallas bore little resemblance to the egoistic, hard-driving, self-centred, and neurotic Bette Davis of 1932. "Tennessee Williams was later to tell us we all needed illusions, and that was one of Bette's," director William Wellman later observed, recalling how difficult it was to tone down Davis's constant wriggling and her particularly awful tendency of squinting while under strong, challenging close-up lighting. Davis and Stanwyck, who was only a year her senior but had already attained huge stardom, got along like oil and water in their few scenes together. "Bette was supposed to be inspired by Barbara's character's example, but it was evident she was jealous because a contemporary had achieved stardom so quickly while she had to grind through small roles and [to date] bad pictures," Wellman remembered a few years later. Barbara detected her jealousy and reacted in classic Stanwyck fashion. While she was not obnoxious to set workers and fellow actors (on the contrary, Stanwyck was known for her pleasant, casual relationships with co-workers), she didn't take bullshit from anyone, having struggled up from Brooklyn in the most difficult of show-business circumstances. Davis' anxious demeanour and frequent fidgeting struck her as staged and intended to hog and, if possible, steal scenes. Davis fumbled her lines and anxiously smoked a cigarette in one scene. "The pace of this scene makes me jittery," she remarked to Stanwyck, who replied, "You make yourself jittery!" Make an effort to fit in!Davis never liked her after that, and the mood was icy. "She's an egotistical little bitch," Stanwyck remarked to Wellman. "For Christ's sake, why doesn't she relax!" She'll get her chance. In Hollywood, there is plenty of room at the top for brilliance."

Later on, when I interviewed Stanwyck, I asked her about various coworkers. She was friendly and welcoming to the majority of them. Her eyes darkened when I mentioned her brief appearances with Davis in So Big. "She was always so driven that you knew she'd make it." "She had a creative ruthlessness that made her success unavoidable," Stanwyck explained. Her tone conveyed the two-edged nature of her remark.

According to the New York Times, "Bette Davis, as a young artist who sees into the complicated story of Selina's life, is unusually competent."

Davis initially collaborated with the actor who would become one of her greatest loves in So Big. While their sequences in So Big were brief, she would have a more intimate encounter with him in the other film in which they appeared concurrently, The Rich Are Always With Us.

George Brent, who was 28 years old in 1932, had a tumultuous and colourful career. Born in Ireland, he came to America when he was eleven years old, after his parents died. Later, he went to Ireland, where he did pieces and walk-ons with the Abbey Theatre while taking on clandestine actions against the British as an Irish revolutionary at the age of seventeen. After narrowly escaping the British, who had a bounty on his head, he was smuggled back to America via ship to Canada in 1921. After odd occupations, he made his acting debut in Canadian stock, then on Broadway, where he was recognized as one of the theatre's most handsome young juveniles in the late 1920s. In 1931, he was noticed by Hollywood and began a long career as a suave, sensual, but uninspired actor who specialises in playing romantic contrast to the likes of Garbo, Loy, and others.

The Rich Are Always With Us starred Ruth Chatterton, Warners' most gorgeous actress-of-the-moment, who had come over from Paramount with a high-paying contract after conquering the talkies in films like Madame X and Sarah and Son. For as long as her Warner reign lasted (only two years, after which her box office plummeted), she was designated in her picture credits as MISS Ruth Chatterton and was dubbed by fan magazines "the Queen" and "The Screen's First Lady." By no means pretty, Ruth had flair, poise, and authority instead, and as one of her admirers wrote, "could sweep in and out of a drawing room with an imperial aplomb that was classy as all-get-" A Broadway star for fifteen years prior to her 1928 screen debut, she had been adored by producer Henry Miller, who called her "Miss Peaches."

Davis encountered this intimidating apparition on her first day on the set of The Rich Are Always With Us. On So Big, Davis found herself silent in a scene with Chatterton, and the star, sensing her bewilderment, took her aside and informed her that she was, after all, a fellow human being and coworker, and that if she relaxed, everything would be fine.

Davis relaxed and had a terrific performance, charmed by Queen Chatterton's democratic approach, who proved big sisterly in comparison to aloof Stanwyck. When I met director Alfred E. Green in the 1950s, he said that Davis appeared to suit the role of Malbro like a glove, a flighty society girl in love with the gorgeous foreign reporter (Brent) whom the married Park Avenue matron (Chatterton) has appropriated for herself. The screenplay was written by an ex-Mr. Miriam Hopkins, Austin Parker, was frothy nonsense about Chatterton's unwavering devotion to a womaniser and rogue par excellence (John Miljan). Brent is angry with her masochistic devotion to Miljan, whom she is divorcing, but they bumble their way to a nice dénouement, sort of.

Chatterton, both on and offscreen, outmanoeuvred Davis in his pursuit of the attractive Mr. Brent. During the filming of The Rich

Are Always With Us, both ladies fell madly in love with him, but it was Chatterton who hurried him off to the altar offscreen as soon as her divorce from her current husband, actor Ralph Forbes, was final.

Surprisingly, losing against Chatterton in the Brent Cupid Sweepstakes did not turn Davis against her. Bette remembers Chatterton's kindnesses to her during the production, and she considered her to be one of the best actresses of her generation.

Davis' later memories of Chatterton may have been sweetened by the knowledge that Chatterton's star was setting as hers rose, and by the fact that Chatterton and Brent's marriage lasted only two years (1932-34), after which Davis would have more than a few digs at him, both on and off screen.

George Brent was an unstable, contemptuous, and sharp-tongued individual. He appeared to have a realistic approach to women, making them dance to his song rather than the other way around. "I will never be owned by a woman; I own myself!"" He once informed producer Hal Wallis that no woman ever established permanent rights to him despite many loves and six marriages, including those to actresses Constance Worth (which lasted only a year, 1937) and Ann Sheridan (who also had a one-year marital turn with him from 1942 to 1943).

Brent had a steadying influence on the ladies in his life and met their problems with a kind of rough compassion that they found healing-while it lasted-despite his rueful realism, sophisticated awareness of the female psyche, and a feet-on-the-ground cynicism doubtless born of his stark and brutal experiences during the Irish rebellion. Davis would greatly benefit from these attributes in the not-too-distant future.

Around this time, Orry-Kelly, born Jack Kelly, began his career as a clothing designer at Warners, and he and cameraman Ernie Haller worked tirelessly to photograph and style Davis to flattering effect. Davis considered herself to be striking rather than attractive at the time (and most people who knew her agreed), but the Haller-Kelly team did wonders with her image in Rich.

The Rich Are Always With Us was panned by the New York Times, which said it "sadly savours more of Hollywood than it does of fashionable New York society." Chatterton was described as "charming," and Davis was pleasantly dismissed and/or patted on the back with "Bette Davis also serves this film well."

Darryl Zanuck kept looking for a suitable lead for Davis and came across The Dark Horse. With a presidential election approaching, Zanuck thought this gubernatorial campaign story had "the right stuff." And the part of the astute, industrious Kay Russell seemed ideal for Davis.

While The Dark Horse will never be considered a classic of the first, or even second, order, it is a vibrant and clever political comedy-drama that best showed Davis.

The plot revolves around her and campaign manager Warren William attempting to sell a gubernatorial candidate (Guy Kibbee) on his colossal ignorance and oafishness. Davis and William strategize their way to an election-night victory for their candidate, while falling solidly in love in the classic leading man-leading lady pattern.

The New York Times praised The Dark Horse, describing Davis as having "a splendid performance" in her first solid major role of the year, and the film itself as "a lively comedy of politics." .."It's full of bright lines and clever incidents, and no word or action is wasted."

In its review, Photoplay described The Dark Horse as a "grand political satire, which comes at the most opportune of moments," adding that "[it] will give you enough chuckles to tide you over a flock of gloomy days."

Meanwhile, Jimmy Quirk, the magazine's editor, was responding to the stream of "Davis looks like Connie Bennett" emails with articles and gossip notes that emphasised the immensely distinctive personalities of both actresses, but favoured Bette. When Connie Bennett visited New York, she encountered Quirk at a party and objected. "You've already made it-you're a big star," he assured her. But she's new and needs any and all kinds of creative publicity. Connie, be a good sport. You have the means to be generous!" Bennett agreed she could afford it, and nothing more was heard from that quarter.

Meanwhile, Davis was having issues with Warren William, a famed ladies' man who allegedly had an erection 90% of the time and had to wear special crotch supports to conceal it-not always effectively. She had avoided his approaches throughout The Dark Horse, only to discover, to her surprise, that Warners expected her to accompany William on a personal appearance tour to New York. She felt Zanuck had concocted this as a favour for William, his friendly opponent in the cocksmanship competition. William made no secret of his sexual attraction to Davis, and she had to object to director Alfred E. Green when he turned their onstage smooching sessions into grope parties.

Davis' talent and potential were appreciated by Zanuck, but she was "too New England staid" for his tastes. "If William has a crush on the dame, I'll make it easy for him," he promised Alfred Green. Davis soon found herself on a train heading east with William and a Warner brigade of publicity guys and administrative staffers.

Davis despised public appearances and publicity tours in 1932. She didn't think she was well known enough yet, and it hurt her vanity to think about people asking, "Who is she?""To her delight, she received the highest level of commendation. "I don't think she realised the enormous exposure Warner films give to even supporting actors," Jack Warner subsequently commented. "The films starring Stanwyck and Chatterton paid off for her."

Davis later credited Warners' hyper efficient publicity machine with propelling her to success. "The disadvantage of the contract system was that we were treated like serfs and were forced to perform roles that were not always appropriate." The benefit was that one got maximum exposure to the public in picture after picture, which was cranked out on a regular basis back then, and beautiful concentrated publicity.``

William didn't seem to mind that Davis was having an affair with Ham Nelson, whom she would marry the following August. "Ham has a bad temper," she suggested. "I know he'll take apart any man who tries to take liberties with me," she said, adding that she planned to go to her married bed as a virgin, which brought nasty laughter from the lusty William. "I can't believe she waited twenty-four years to find out what a guy had in his pants and what he did with it!"He snorted at Zanuck. "She's spewing a lot of horseshit." Back in high school, she was undoubtedly into the lads' pants!"

Zanuck was surprised to see himself defending a lady for a change. "She didn't go to a high school, she went to an academy," he clarified, "and I don't know any guy who made her, but you can try your luck if you want!""

Warren William, once in New York with his wary prey, devised a sketch for him and Davis to perform at the Capitol Theater, with Zanuck's agreement. It was titled The Burglar and the Lady and depicted a burglary that was later revealed to be a spoof simulating a movie scene, with the director crying, "Cut!"

But "cut" was not to be back at the hotel, where Davis and William got rooms on the same level (again, courtesy to the clever Zanuck). When Davis heard the pattern of small feet out in the corridor too often and heard Warren's unmistakable, sexy voice calling out, "Room service!" She dialled Ham's number. "I believe I am in imminent danger of being raped." Make something of it!"

Mr. Warren William received a phone call from an irate Ham within ten minutes. "Who do you think you are, making time for MY woman?"" was the least of Mr. Nelson's remarks to Mr. William, and after that, all was pretty quiet at both the hotel and the theatre. "I couldn't escape Warren's looks, at any rate," Davis subsequently said. "They claim that appearances can kill. Believe me when I say that looks can undress!"

Bette Davis has stated that her favourite line from her next picture, Cabin in the Cotton, is "I'd love to kiss ya, but I just washed my hair!"" Of course, she said this in the southern accent she developed for the picture, which starred a pretty washed-out-looking Richard Barthelmess. His popularity as the well-meaning innocent forced to display his manhood under pressure had passed during the sophisticated Depression age of gangsters and guys who beat women around and made them like it, and his career would end a few years later.

Michael Curtiz was the film's hesitant director. He didn't want Davis to play Madge, the attractive planter's daughter who seduces sharecropper's son Barthelmess in the midst of a planter-sharecropper feud. During filming, he humiliated Davis in whatever way he could, calling her "a no-good sexless son of a bitch" and pestering her with similar obscenities as she was making love to a camera without Barthelmess to play to.

Darryl Zanuck insisted that Davis be able to conjure the steamy eroticism required for the role. Curtiz lacked the courtesy to accept his error even after he was proven wrong during filming.

Davis knew Madge was a big part of her, so she gave it her best.

Davis undresses in a closet and emerges clearly naked in a renowned bedroom seduction scene, despite the fact that the shots are captured at shoulder height. She moves on Barthelmess, who is excited by her approach and brokenly whispers her name as the scenario melts into a passionate hug.

The scene-and Davis's overall performance-is all the more amazing because Davis was still a virgin, with her wedding only a few weeks away. Perhaps it was her frustration with that situation, her desperation to be free of it, that brought the scene such intensity and sexual kineticism.

In 1960, a few years before his death from cancer, I interviewed Richard Barthelmess, and one of the issues we discussed was Davis's ascension as seductress supreme in Cabin in the Cotton. "I felt she was emerging from some kind of chrysalis, that true womanhood had somehow eluded her up to then, that family pressures, her mother, her puritanical upbringing, had somehow kept her in delayed adolescence," she added. "She exuded a lot of passion, and it was impossible not to sense it." She was twenty-four at the time, and there was a lot of emotion trapped in her, a lot of electricity that hadn't yet found an outlet. It was disconcerting and, yes, frightening in some ways."

"I was thirty-seven or so at the time, and had forgotten a lot more than she was in the process of discovering-and I don't mean acting," Barthelmess continued. I admit that I was never known as a sexy lover-boy, onstage or off. That was not my thing, my talent, if you will, but she was so fascinating and alluring that she would have aroused a wooden Indian.

"More importantly, she was an excellent actress who, even back then, I knew only needed the right director and script to shine alongside the best stars of the time." When Of Human Bondage came out a few years later, I wasn't surprised by the buzz she created.

Cabin had it all, but the plot and director were not suitable for her."

Curtiz had gone out of his way to be rude to Davis, according to Barthelmess. "He'd fought Zanuck over her casting, probably thinking Ann Dvorak or another directly sexual type would have been more appropriate, and he couldn't admit it when he realised he'd been wrong." Mike Curtiz was a jerk. I was the star of the film, so I could ignore him and retreat to my dressing room, but Bette was a contract player who had to put up with him, and she did. She did, in fact, taunt him at times. Darryl Zanuck believed in her, and Curtiz couldn't get rid of her. And she gave it her all in that performance."

Cabin in the Cotton was Davis's breakthrough performance. When the film was released in late September 1932, critics immediately recognized Davis's new persona. The New York American's Regina Crewe raved about "that flashy, luminous newcomer Bette Davis, who romps off with first honours, for hers is the most dashing and colourful role." Crewe ended her rave review with, "The girl is superb." Richard Watts, Jr. of The New York Herald-Tribune noted, "Miss Davis shows a surprising vivacity as the seductive rich girl."

She might have used that help badly, because Warner and Zanuck did not invest in her. In her next film, Three on a Match, she appeared for about 15 minutes of the 63-minute running length. Warren William, her adversary, was also present to harass and bother her. "I think you'd be flattered by Warren's attention," one of her co-stars, Ann Dvorak, told her. "If you like him so much, he's yours on a silver platter," Davis retorted. Joan Blondell was also in the film about three girls, one a former reform school inmate (Blondell) who turns entertainer; another a wealthy matron (Dvorak) with a little son she adores-and the third, Davis, a drab secretarial-school graduate who works as a stenographer (Davis-a stenographer) and is given no story line (she seems to be on hand only to join the other two in lighting from the same match in a restaurant scene, hence the title). According to superstition, the third person to use the match will die, which turns out to be Dvorak, who breaks her marriage and destroys herself with alcohol and drugs. Blondell is the heir to both the spouse and the son. Davis, on the other hand, disappears without a trace after serving as a sort of friend to the kid while all the melodrama is ironed out-a thankless role in a thankless picture for the formerly hot siren of Cabin in the Cotton. Warren William was less rakish and more respectable than normal as the spouse who eventually finds solace in Blondell, and because his interactions with Davis were nearly nonexistent, his advances were infrequent-at least on set.

Davis was furious at being pushed into Match after performing so brightly in Cotton. She reminded everyone that it was a classic illustration of the poisonous contract system in which a player had to accept whatever was allocated or face punishment. She was especially irritated since the screenwriter, Lucien Hubbard, had left her with no juicy moments to play and had even denied her a romantic interest! Mervyn LeRoy, engrossed as he was in making Joan Blondell and Ann Dvorak look as thrilling as possible, was no assistance as director.

Davis recalled years later, with bitter irony, how LeRoy had told her, tactlessly, that he thought Joan Blondell would become "a great star" and Ann Dvorak's potential was "unlimited." "Great for them—but what about me?"" was her initial reaction. "It wasn't that I didn't wish the other girls well," she went on, "but I didn't get a crumb out of that script!""The ultimate irony was that neither Dvorak nor Blondell ever came close to Davis's great stardom." The critics were quick to point out Davis's abuse during the match. Among other things, the critic of Hollywood Filmograph commented that "Bette Davis is ravishing in appearance, but had very little to do."But in real life, she was set to co-star in a significant part. Ham Nelson has returned-and he was here to stay.

5.

Ham, Sex, and Other Things

I WAS SURELY PURITAN! Helpless enthusiasm!"This is how Bette Davis described herself during the hot summer of 1932 in her memoirs." She had taken on her mother's subliminal views and focused all her sexual energy into her job, playing out scenarios in movies that in sophisticated terms were far ahead of the mother-and-sister-preoccupied life she actually led at twenty-four.

Ham Nelson then reappeared. After working as a trumpeter in nightclubs in the East, he came to Hollywood to play in a band associated with the Olympics, which were staged in Los Angeles that summer. He soon got a position at the Colony Club, where he played trumpet in the jazz band.

Ham hadn't changed much since she first met him at Cushing Academy when he was sixteen. He was now twenty-four years old, yet he was still the same shy, insecure, gangling introvert he had always been. He sought solace in his music, attacking the trumpet like a demon. Ruthie regarded Ham well. He'd make an excellent son-in-law, she reasoned. His familial and New England roots were equal to those of Favour and Davis. He and Davis got along well; there was some physical chemistry between them; he was polite and serious; and he had taught Davis a lot about music, not just jazz but also classical.

Ruthie started bugging Bette about how she was twenty-four and in risk of becoming a bachelor girl converted into an old maid if she waited any longer to marry. Davis listened half-jokingly, half-seriously. It was true that she considered her virginity to be a burden. She'd been playing steamy love scenes on stage and television for four years, with a variety of guys, but she hadn't known a man in the biblical sense, and her curiosity and physical desires were growing. She kept joking that all she actually knew about naked men was what she was compelled to address when she diapered the youngster in that early film. At home, she and Bobby devoured medical and anatomy texts, becoming well-versed in the "facts" of male-female intercourse. But the sixty-four-dollar inquiry was, "How did it feel?" And did it feel any different with a man you loved versus a man you were just drawn to?

Davis had plenty of time to contemplate Ham's potential as a husband and lover because he was on hand, subject to daily examination (with his clothes on, of course). She admired his sensitivity, musicianship, and cautious, tentative demeanour. She thought it was strange that a man who had played with so many orchestras in so many places didn't convey more fiery, outgoing toughness and hardiness. She concluded that Ham had grown more attractive over the years. She knew he didn't think so—he'd described himself as "a big, gawky loon"—but she found his tallness and still-adolescent clumsiness endearing. He told her he thought his nose was too wide and his mouth was too thick, but she thought they added character and intrigue to his face.

She and Bobby speculated on Ham's sexual encounter. Has he ever dated a woman? They read that if they weren't lustful girl chasers, young males who weren't married masturbated regularly. Was Ham maybe a male virgin? He wasn't saying anything, and she wasn't asking. What had happened to Ham in the intervening eight years? Why were the lives of young men so mysterious to women? Why was it forced to be this way?

Davis finally asked Ham whether he was ready to marry, prodded on by Ruthie, who asserted emphatically that it was time she functioned as a woman. She was never willing to say in later years that she had proposed, but she had, with Ruthie poking away in the background.

Ham agreed right away.

Ruthie, as usual, recommended the date, location, and terms of the wedding, which was held on August 18, 1932. She left Ham, her mother, and Bobby for Yuma, Arizona, still apprehensive and unsure, conscious that Ruthie was speeding things to keep her from altering her mind. They chose Arizona because California required a six-week waiting period. Davis had no plans for romantic aeroplane flights, which were already fashionable in 1932. They set out in a beat-up Auburn that threatened to conk out at any minute along the dusty pre-freeway roads.

The heat of the desert was lethal. There were few and far between gas stations. As they sweated profusely in the heat, their garments adhered to them. Davis drove as Ham sat alongside her, languishing and wretched, while Ruthie and Bobby sweated and whined in the back. They checked into a second-rate hotel in Yuma after a painful voyage of several hours, dried their clothing, and Ham went out to buy a suit and wedding ring—a cheap one, because Yuma's few stores were hardly a class act, even by 1932 standards.

An Indian missionary married them the next morning. According to Ruthie, Ham misplaced the ring twice: once through a hole in his pocket, and the other time it slid into a floor crack and he had to grovel to get it. They returned to California and Zuma Beach, where Davis was living, immediately after the uninspired, perfunctory ceremony.

Davis waxed rhapsodic in her memoirs about what transpired after she and her bridegroom had scented and lotioned themselves to the nines, gotten rid of Ruthie and Bobby, shut the door of their room, and climbed into bed for the first time as husband and wife. "This was Ruth Elizabeth's golden moment," Davis says. The happiness of a wedding night has arrived. Hers was the relationship under God and everything between a man and an honest-to-goodness maid, and her joy was limitless. ...Passion is codified, love is ritualised, and sex is tolerated by society."

Davis continued, becoming more descriptive (for her), if still restrained: "I was able to shower an object with the unnamed joy that lay simmering beneath my humourless drive without a trace of guilt, with no fear of disapproval."

Many years later, Davis described the night to Jerry Asher in more realistic terms, lamenting that she had no affairs before marriage and expressing envy of young women in the 1960s who could "try a guy out, see if he fit for size." If she had been a virgin that night of August 18, 1932, she discovered that Ham was a chronic masturbator, was given to premature ejaculation, was shy and awkward, and even unsure of which orifices She added that as the years passed, she began to wonder about Ham's sexuality, wondering if he had had brief and hesitant relationships with other male musicians on his national tours. Bobby subsequently told her that when men were put together, they often engaged in casual relations- was this a part of her bridegroom's background, she wondered?

She claimed that, despite her lack of experience, she had to be the sexual aggressor, that, owing to the medical and anatomical manuals she and her sister had studied, she brought Ham to climax, but she couldn't get him "properly trained" to satisfy her until months after they married. She even revealed that Ham's tall, rangy form, highly muscled and well endowed in the critical region, had so enthralled her that she had not hesitated to masturbate and even fellate him—practices deemed wicked in the extreme in 1932, and not only by puritans like her mother. Later, she remembered his total, abandoned enjoyment of these acts as suspicious, ominous. ...She did, however, concede that once she had encouraged and coached him in more penetrative missionary-position techniques, he performed admirably.

However, she spoke to Ham in largely negative terms years later, along the lines of "you never know anyone until you're married to him." There was his whining, his meek willingness to do the dishes and make the beds rather than protesting that it was a woman's job, his moodiness and pouting, his unwillingness to play the man's role. She desired a decisive, forceful, macho man on whom she could lean, defer, one who would dominate her and set the course of their life. Ham, she claimed, had failed her badly. There was an imbalance in their wages that embarrassed him. And the time difference—as Ham went to bed after a night of playing in a band, she got up to go to the studio. Bette gradually lost respect for Ham Nelson as a result of his silences, withdrawal, unwillingness to stand up to Ruthie and Bobby, who had taken up residence behind the house she and Ham rented, his tendency to walk away from a confrontation, and his almost feminine languor.

Davis gradually found that she was married to three persons rather than one between the years 1932-1935. There was Ham, who alternated between whimpering self-pity and outright aggression. He would first cry, then strike her. She camped out with him in auto courts and cooked for him when he was on tour with his band—that is, if she wasn't in a picture. Her attempts to play the role of the tiny wife irritated him. His efforts to clean and wash dishes made him appear weak and feminine to her. He then began boxing to become more forceful. However, he overcompensated by becoming overly confrontational, knocking around other men, such as Ross Alexander, who expressed interest in his wife. He felt himself as a cuckold, with rivals lurking around every turn.

Davis detected Ham's fragility despite his boxing gloves and tough bravado. She gradually lost respect for him, and even started to loathe him, but she refused to recognize she had failed in what she saw as a woman's most essential role—marriage. Ham was a symbol of her dedication, and as such, he had to be supported and endured.

Davis frantically tried to relive the first year or so of their marriage, the romantic love they had known in fits and starts amidst her boy-man spouse's sex education and bashful, anxious bumblings. She was confident in his musical ability, but she was disappointed that his desire didn't even come close to matching hers. He lived paycheck to paycheck and took no initiative to acquire higher band spots. Whatever did arrive seemed to come by chance rather than any great motivation on Ham's side. One of his few advantages was that he appeared to be faithful to her. "But what other woman would want him then?"" Ruthie remarked mockingly. Because there seemed to be no strong reason to dissolve the marriage, it dragged on through 1933, 1934, 1935, and beyond.

Then there were the other two "wives" Davis had married, Ruthie and Bobby.

Davis often reflected on her practice of portraying herself as the "husband," the "man of the house," to her three children. She always came to the same conclusion. She had taken over the job left vacant by Harlow Morrell Davis when she was seven years old. It didn't take a psychoanalyst to figure that out, she grumbled.

Ruthie was kept in fine homes, fine clothes, maids, and beautiful furbelows now that she had the money and resources. Davis had only one servant, Dell Pfeiffer, a devoted, long-suffering, friendly black lady who adored Davis and even enjoyed her furious outbursts and frequent temper tantrums. Dell has little regard for the Three Wives. She avoided ham. Ruthie, she was quite quiet. And Bobby frightened her.

Now that Davis had "arrived," Ruthie felt entitled to the best because she was Bette Davis's mother. Davis had to make sacrifices in order to keep her mother in comfort. Ruthie walked in front of Davis at premieres and other public events. Bobby reportedly said, "You'd think she was the movie star and Bette was just an afterthought."

Bobby was the final straw. Bobby, consumed by sibling rivalry, declared in 1932 that she, too, wished to be an actress, but because she lacked the discipline to train and the talent to act, doors were barred to her, despite Davis' admittedly half-hearted efforts to pull strings. Bobby then went on a string of marriages, all of which failed miserably. She had a serious self-image problem. Bette is the favourite, she used to say as a child. I wanted what Better had; I wanted to be Better.

Bobby began to slip into emotional problems that eventually turned into terrible, all-out mental diseases when she realised she would never be Better, or even come within a mile of her in any way. Her only child, Faye, a sorrowful girl who lived in the shadow of her unstable mother and a series of short-term stepfathers, she sighed, was the only positive thing she had contributed to the world. Bobby began to move in and out of a series of pricey private sanitariums, depleting Davis's resources significantly. Bobby had succeeded Ruthie as parasite king. It was a character she would play for the next four decades. Bette and Ruthie took turns caring for Faye when Bobby was "indisposed."

Bobby came to work as a housekeeper for Davis on occasion over those years, when she was feeling better, especially when new medicines kept her somewhat balanced. Davis, enraged at the drain her sister and mother represented, frequently used Bobby as a butt for her increasingly ferocious frustrations and rages. At times, Davis would lavish love and apologies on this beleaguered sibling, who felt being Bette Davis's sister a terrible psychological weight.

Davis had previously considered her visits to Bobby's psychiatric facilities to be an unbearable hardship. She frequently found her in an open ward, alone and despondent. Doctors would confidently advocate state facilities, telling Davis that they provided superior care than the private sanitariums for whom Davis was paying exorbitant, extortionate costs. Bobby's spouse, Faye's father, Robert

Pelgram, had fled to divorce court. It was all too much for this quiet, retiring man.

Davis will never forget a trip to "the Bobby Bughouse," as she dubbed it. She was sitting calmly, urging Bobby to eat a cupcake from the box of treats she had brought, when three female inmates from The Snake Pit walked in. They continued, half-flatteringly, half-derisively, to give manic imitations of Davis to her face, swishing around with swivelling hips and holding imaginary smokes at unusual angles, and popping their eyes outlandishly, shocked and delighted by the sight of Bette Davis Herself in their midst. "They were silent performances," Davis subsequently explained. "At the very least, they didn't yowl, 'Petah—the lettah!'"""

Davis had three wives like this.

Meanwhile, her "husband" continued to work on her films with maniacal focus.

Darryl Zanuck believed that Davis could play Fay in 20,000 Years in Sing Sing alongside Spencer Tracy. Tracy was borrowed from Fox to play Tom Connors, a confident mobster confined to Sing Sing on a felony conviction and believes his powerful underworld buddies will rescue him via speedy parole. Davis, as his girlfriend, portrayed a female who appeared tough and entrepreneurial on the outside but had her own flaws.

Davis was excited about the character, which she felt had more depth than most, and she put herself into the role of Fay. True, she had martinet Michael Curtiz jumping on her again, but because he now sensed her ability after her Cabin in the Cotton reviews, he tended to give her more respect—and less attention, because he was directing one of those hard, tough, brutal "men's dramas" that he greatly enjoyed and excelled at.

Davis, largely left to her own devices, fulfilled Zanuck's hopes for her by making her characterization real and vivid—her achievement all the more remarkable given that she found herself awash in a sea of melodramatic "men's stuff." Davis had always admired Spencer Tracy, who, incidentally, shared her birthday, April 5, despite being eight years her senior—at the time, thirty-two to her twenty-four. She'd seen him on stage and in his early films, and she'd always wanted to work with him. Tracy, who was quiet and humble in his underplaying acting technique, could pack a lot of conviction into his "art that concealed art," and Davis took advantage of every opportunity to observe his work when she wasn't acting alongside him.

"Tracy was one of those men she thoroughly respected from start to finish," said Louis Calhern, who played a character in the film. "It wasn't so much a sexual attraction as it was one strong spirit's admiration for her counterpart." And the admiration was returned in full."

Tracy thought Davis was a terrific player with limitless potential, and they had off-set morale-boosting conversations. As of late 1932, neither of them was getting the parts their talents deserved, and Tracy traded stories of Fox miscastings in cheap, badly done films with his, sympathising especially when she raved about being "shunted aside in a nothing role" in Three on a Match—a film she never let the Warners powers that be forget.

When asked years later why Tracy and Davis didn't fall in love while filming 20,000 Years in Sing Sing, Michael Curtiz answered, "They were too similar, did too much identifying with each other." I suppose Tracy, as much as he respected her, was turned off by her male toughness and feistiness, and as for her—well, he was a fairly plain man for all his dynamism, and I felt she preferred 'em more attractive-like George Brent, for example."

They continued to be friends in first-rate form, talking about the great movies they would do together when they were "rich and famous," however they never did another film together, though they did do a radio show-of one of her best hits, Dark Victory.

Warden Lewis E. Lawes' book about prison circumstances inspired the film 20,000 Years in Sing Sing, which starred Arthur Byron as Warden Long. It was a tough, realistic novel that inspired a tough, realistic film. Tracy, who was haughty initially, is humbled by his difficult prison experiences, including weeks in solitary confinement. Later, his adjustment to prison life improves, and when he learns that Fay, the Davis character, has been in an automobile accident, he is granted a brief furlough to visit her, with the assurance that he will return at a specified time on his own recognizance. He gets into a fight with the mobster (the Calhern character) who sent him to prison in Fay's bedroom, and accepts responsibility for Day after she shoots his adversary. He is later sentenced to death via electric chair. (Of fact, under stricter Production Code decisions implemented a year later, in 1934, Fay would have had to pay for her own crime.)

The New York Times' Mordaunt Hall appreciated the Tracy-Davis co-starrer enough, stating, "In this rapidly-paced film, there are some extraordinarily interesting glimpses of prison routine." ...Spencer Tracy is an actor. ..He remarked, "Bette Davis does well as Fay."

20,000 Years in Sing Sing does not hold up well in recent years, with plot devices that are maudlin and unbelievable by modern standards, though the cast, which includes Warren Hymer, Grant Mitchell, and Louis Calhern, does well, and Curtiz keeps the action moving despite the illogic of some of the situations.

Louis Calhern, a brilliant Broadway actor who subsequently became a renowned character performer in films and performed Shakespeare's King Lear on the stage to acclaim, told me in 1954 that 20,000 Years in Sing Sing was typical of the fast-paced Depression dramas of the early 1930s. "None of us were meant to shine in our roles-we were defeated by the material." We were there to serve the plot situations; there was little time for real characterization, and action, movement, and excitement were essential-which is where Mike Curtiz and the writers came in.

"Mike was a great director for this type of frantic action, but he was a difficult and temperamental man to work with." I know Bette and Tracy both thought he was a pain in the neck. Of all, he didn't dare to be disrespectful to Tracy-at least not beyond a certain point, otherwise Tracy would have hauled off and hit him. Bette wasn't afraid to yell back at him, snarl, and even spit at him if he went too far. Mike probably enjoyed encouraging her."

Davis was then hustled into Parachute Jumper, a film starring Douglas Fairbanks, Jr. It would be the only time they ever acted together (though he would subsequently be involved as a producer in one of her film projects).

In his latest memoirs, Fairbanks dismisses both Davis and the film in a few words. Davis deemed him arrogant because he was "Pickfair royalty," the son of legendary swashbuckler Douglas, Sr. and Mary Pickford's stepson. He was also Joan Crawford's spouse, despite the fact that their marriage was falling apart due to mutual infidelities—hers with Clark Gable, who was married at the time—not that anyone cared.

Humiliated at home, Fairbanks was apathetic, cynical, and arrogant toward Hollywood and Hollywood people in early 1933. Later that year, while they filmed Morning Glory, he fell in love with Katharine Hepburn (as he later admitted in his book). He received no reaction from the lady despite his efforts. His crush for Hepburn is evident in a number of moments in which he listens to her problems in such a sympathetically concerned manner that it sparked suspicion about his affections for her even at the time. Within a year, he'd be off to England, where he'd spend several years, becoming, as Davis later remarked, "more British than the British."

While they would become friends-sort-of-many years later, Fairbanks and Davis' chemistry was lacking in simpatico in 1933, and their scenes together demonstrate their mutual disinterest all too clearly. "Those love scenes between them were the stiffest kind I'd ever had to deal with," director Alfred E. Green subsequently remarked. "I used to laugh because the film was based on a true story called Some Call It Love." All I can say is that no one would have confused it for love the way they two played it!"

Davis was dissatisfied with everything about Parachute Jumper in her circa-1933 discontented and irritated manner. She didn't think photographer Jim Van Trees lit her properly or highlighted her best angles; she thought Green overlooked her for the male actors; she found the talented Leo Carrillo irritating and claimed he tried to pinch her; and she and Claire Dodd, a cut-rate femme fatale supporting player, rubbed each other the wrong way—especially when she noted Claire got better clothes to wear and better photography. "The damned cameraman had a crush on her—at my expense!"" she snorted later.

As Fairbanks' sidekick, Frank McHugh, who was given the absurd name "Toodles," later said that the mood on the set was tight and uncomfortable, and everyone was eager to get it over with, especially Green, who had to keep them all out of each other's hair.

"Bette was going through a tense and miserable period, and I understood why," McHugh stated at the time. "She was getting knocked around in one man's picture after another, and she wasn't getting enough chances to shine." And it irritated her and made her grumpy." On set, she and McHugh reminisced about their stock days.

Fairbanks had an annoying habit of letting Davis's tensions and snappishness wash over him. As Green recalled, he frequently treated her as if she didn't exist. "He regarded her as the standard 'love interest' necessary to the plot line for, in his view, some idiotic reason, and she was someone to be tolerated and disregarded whenever possible."

The film is a joke about pilots drafted to fly narcotics into the US, with Fairbanks, once a naval flyer, exposing the villains of drug lord Carrillo and eventually handing him over to authorities. Davis plays "Alabama," a southern girl who has "gone wild in New York," and she worked hard to perfect her accent. Weekly Variety's observation rewarded her. "[Miss Davis] has a Southern accent that gets across," said a sceptical Times critic. .."speaks with a decided Southern drawl," he says, but he doesn't say whether he approves or disapproves.

Davis was thrilled to be cast in a film called The Working Man alongside her former mentor and career catalyst, George Arliss. Arliss noticed right away that her self-assurance and self-possession had grown dramatically in the year since The Man Who Played God. "My little bird has escaped her cage and found her wings," he told her after their first scene.

She then learnt that Arliss had specifically demanded that Warner and Zanuck cast her in his film. He had continued to take a fatherly interest in her worries and anxieties, and he wanted to see for himself her improvement in cinema technique. He approached photographer Sol Polito and requested him to favour Davis in as many images as possible, and even went so far as to debate her clothes with Orry-Kelly, who, talented man that he was, sometimes inclined to overkill, overshadowing his actresses with his ingenuity. Arliss also collaborated with director John Adolfi to accentuate Davis's greatest traits, and the result is slick, authoritative, and fierce.

"I always sensed that Mr. Arliss was one hundred percent in my corner, as he was in that first film, and I shall always be grateful to him," Davis stated at the time. She went on to say that Arliss had taught her "something wonderful" about film acting, which she never forgot: "Films are not shot in situational continuity, so always keep in mind the action in the scene just before and after, at least as they appear in the script progression." Believe me, Mr. Arliss' advice saved my life!"

Arliss, an Academy Award winner who was as foresighted in directing as he was in playing, gently urged her not to give too much of herself in sequences of minor importance. "He was right about that, too," Davis subsequently said. "I went into each and every scene, at least in that period, on all cylinders, sometimes lending them an intensity and an attack beyond the merits of the situation."

The Working Man was a mediocre effort unworthy of Arliss, Davis, and the other performers. In it, Arliss is a retired shoemaker who accepts an incognito position at a competing firm because he is restless and wants to assist the scions of his deceased competition to shape up and fly before they lose their inheritance due to their frivolous lives. He soon finds himself competing with his stuffed-shirt nephew (Hardie Albright), whom he had placed in control of his own business—and of course, the mischievous heirs, Davis and Theodore Newton, see the mistake of their ways.

Davis had issues with the attractive young Theodore Newton, who played her brother. Newton refused to accept her protests that she was a "settled married woman and thus now beyond the pale," and began following her around, bringing her coffee on set, and otherwise waxing "uncomfortably attentive." She mentioned this to Arliss, who scoffed, "Oh the boy has a crush—and let him work it out by being nice and understanding." He's not going to hurt you." "I'm not sure—you haven't seen the glitter in that kid's eye," she snapped back. Adolfi and Albright spoke with the frustrated would-be swain at her request, and he proceeded to cool off as best he could. "Thank God he plays my brother and there are no love scenes," she relieved Albright, who smiled, "He may surprise you with some incest ideas yet!"" However, a word to the wise was sufficient, and Newton kept his distance.

Davis had some wonderful critical pats on the back as a result of all the care and attention Arliss had ensured for her. "Good work," the Times said. "Strong scores," stated the Film Daily critic.

Bette and Ham were offered a free honeymoon in early 1933, but it was an unusual one. They were sent out with the Forty-second Street Special, a round-the-country train tour that stopped in every major city where the opulent new musical Forty-second Street was premiering. Warners and General Electric split the expense of the elaborately outfitted and staffed Pullman train, which arrived in Washington for Franklin D. Roosevelt's inauguration in March 1933.

In thirty-two days, they visited thirty-two cities. Glenda Farrell, Laura La Plante, Joe E. Brown, Olympic star Eleanor Holm, Tom Mix and his horse—who had his own car—Leo Carrillo, and Preston Foster were among those escorting Bette and Ham, who felt a little bewildered amid all the great names. A dozen lovely chorus girls were also on hand, eliciting wolf whistles at every turn. Fans stared wide-eyed at them, and some hooted at all the glitter—after all, it was the depths of the Great Depression, and the new President Roosevelt would soon close the banks. Scrip was used as a money replacement in Boston. Davis and Ham met members of the Roosevelt family in Washington—she was a staunch supporter of the new president—and then it was on to New York and yet another procession, with much smiling and waving to many tattered, lonely people. Davis noted that it was then she understood Hollywood converted even minor characters into household names—those garbage pictures she had endured were not to be dismissed as a total loss after all.

She remembered that sex was the last thing on her and Ham's minds amid all of the excitement and uncomfortable train travels. When Ham returned to Los Angeles and his household habits were restored, his sexual quirks served their customary purpose—for him. Davis learned in retrospect that his masturbatory practices, which she knew he continued alone, were being adapted for other goals, including the prevention of any possible pregnancy. To her chagrin and despair, one of Ham's talents was coitus interruptus, as did his failure to "hold his fire" until her orgasm approached or matched his own. At the last second, he'd pull out and shoot his sperm on her leg-it was sticky, but it worked. She initially assumed it was an accident, a byproduct of his still gauche libido. He was doing it on purpose, she realised. She eventually talked him out doing it, but he subsequently started wearing condoms. She said they inflamed her vaginal lining, deceived him into going without them a couple times, and then became pregnant.

Davis was confronted with some difficult questions after duping Ham into prospective fatherhood without giving it much thought. Did she truly want a baby at the age of twenty-five, with her career on the rise? Could she take a break? Her desire to be a mother was at odds with her strong careerism. Ham and Ruthie quickly took advantage of her ambiguity.

When she told Ham she was pregnant, his face was solemn and solemn. He suggested she was too busy to have a baby; her work would suffer as a result. He would not be "humiliated" if she had to pay the hospital fees. If he wasn't financially successful enough to pay for his own child's birth, he should postpone. Abortion was unavoidable! Then Ruthie wrote from the East, where she was attending Bobby during one of her recurring nervous breakdowns, saying she agreed with Ham. It was awful for her work, too "cluttery," and too inconvenient.

Davis went with Ham to a scruffy little quack in a dusty little house in a dreary little town fifty miles from L.A., resigned on the outside but torn and miserable on the inside. Ham waited in the car outside. It just took around one hour. She drove home in hushed stillness with him, but afterward went into the bathroom and screamed for an hour. Even married people faced a stigma when it came to abortion in 1933. With the medical risks-infection, blood loss-many women died as a result. Davis aborted twice, avoiding the worst-case scenario.

6.

Battling Toward the Big Break

Davis has some harsh words in her autobiography about her next picture, Ex-Lady. She describes it as follows:

"Darryl Zanuck [inspired by the critical and popular support for Davis's recent efforts] decided it was time to give me the glamour-star treatment." It was a huge blunder. I wasn't the kind to be glamorised in the traditional sense. I was made over and cast as the star of a piece of rubbish called Ex-Lady, which was supposed to be controversial and pushed everyone of sensibility to nausea in an ecstasy of bad taste and a burst of wasted energy.

"My avant-garde lover was Gene Raymond, whom I eventually dumped for the marvellously corrupt Monroe Owsley." One disgruntled critic [from the Hollywood Reporter] claimed that Warner Brothers might have saved money by photographing the entire film on one bed. It's a component of my job that I try to avoid as much as possible. My shame was only compounded by my wrath from the daily filming to the billboards, which erroneously depicted me half-naked." Robert Florey's pedestrian direction was no help either.

It is unusual that Davis, who aspired to popularity, would object to having her name appear above the title of a film. Ex-Lady's plot, a retread of Barbara Stanwyck's 1931 film Illicit, was not only interesting and refreshing in those pre-Production Code days, but also decades ahead of its time. Davis portrayed a free-spirited individual who believed in living with her lover without the privilege of marriage, which she felt killed the romance and encouraged all sorts of sterility and monotony.

The plot facts from the Stanwyck film, as repeated by David Boehm with new speech and circumstances, were superficial, implausible, and too neatly telescoped and tied up. Then there's reason to suspect Davis hated being given a reworked version of a Barbara Stanwyck star vehicle; she'd despised Stanwyck since So Big.

In addition, column items suggested that she and Gene Raymond, her handsome, sexy co-star (later the longtime husband of Jeanette McDonald and a breezy, blond charmer who was great with the ladies), seemed to enjoy each other's company excessively and exclusively on the set, despite the fact that she had only been married six months.

The advertising, however, was what truly turned her off the film; one of the full-page ads that Warners put in fan magazines and other national newspapers showed her allegedly naked from the breasts up, fully made up, and glaring forth with brazen provocativeness. The legend above her face read: WE DON'T DARE TELL YOU HOW DARING IT IS! "Never before has the screen had the courage to present a story so frank—so outspoken—yet so true!" it said on the side. Prepare for a sensational surprise!"

Some commentators irritated her by claiming she had been stared over the title too soon; she wasn't ready. She believed they missed the point that if she had starred in a worthy film, her popularity would have been well-deserved.

Davis and Raymond are coworkers at an advertising agency in the story—he is a writer, she is a commercial artist. She is adamantly opposed to marriage as a stultifying, unromantic institution, and he reluctantly agrees with her until career demands drive them to marry. Money problems and attempted infidelities ensue, he with Kay Strozzi, she with Monroe Owsley. They eventually settle for a sham reconciliation in which 1933 middle-class delusions are calmed by the suggestion that marriage is not that bad after all.

In 1974, Davis told one of her biographers, Whitney Stine, "I don't think a more unsuitable part in a cheaper type film could have been found to launch me into stardom." It was a calamity."

As Davis's would-be seducer, the "marvellously corrupt" Owsley was one of the film's main assets. He provided an almost refreshing contrast to super wholesome yet attractive, all-American blond Gene Raymond in his sinister, sickly, rat-faced character. Offscreen, Owsley was a bizarre, tortured man who had many traits with another oddity, Colin Clive, who appeared alongside Davis in a later film. Owsley was the subject of a slew of frightening rumours, ranging from reports of his intense gay seductions to scandals involving drug usage, alcoholism, and gambling. Whatever his personal difficulties, Owsley was one of the few actors who could express his complete self, grim as it was, on screen with theatrical flair and panache. While Davis agreed that "this rat-faced rodent gives me the shivers," she was the first to admit that whatever he conveyed was perfectly successful on video. The reasons for Owsley's death remain unknown, and there were reports that the studio kept the most dramatic aspects of his death under wraps.

One letter published in a fan magazine described Owsley as "a slimy toad, a no-good rat up to trouble—and you feel he's like that off-camera, too!""It was significant that Owsley did not sue the magazine for libel—he almost certainly agreed with every word of it!"

The following is an excerpt from the New York Times review:

"Bette Davis, a young actress who has demonstrated intelligence in the roles that have been assigned to her in films, has had the misfortune of being cast in the lead role of Ex-Lady." That somewhat sinister event meant to her employers that Miss Davis, having demonstrated the necessary aptitude and pictorial attraction, had now become a star in her own right. Miss Davis had to spend an uncomfortable amount of time en déshabillé in boudoir scenes, engaged in repartee and behaviour that were sometimes timidly suggestive, then depressingly naive, and mostly downright foolish, according to her embarrassed admirers at the Strand on Thursday night."

"I felt the film was ahead of its time, and Bette looked just wonderful in it," Gene Raymond told me many years later. She had a great photographer [Tony Gaudio] for that. I had a lot of fun on set with the other performers, especially Frank McHugh, Claire Dodd, and Bette, though Bette was so serious and passionate that she made us all look like amateurs in contrast. I did detest some ridiculous publicity that implied we were set on each other—especially since she was married—because I needed an irate spouse breathing down my neck like I needed a head cold, but we tried to laugh it off as mere fluff designed to sell a movie."

"I know Bette was unhappy with the film—she told both Pat O'Brien and me she was—but it wasn't all that bad, and there was some snappy dialogue in it, though maybe I'm looking at it from my angle because I had a lot to say!" Frank McHugh remarked."

Davis and Robert Florey did not get along, possibly because neither had much faith in the material. "If they decided they wanted her to be a full-fledged Warner star," Florey later told Adela Rogers St. Johns, "they could have showcased her in something better than that." Davis couldn't agree more.

Davis' only genuine enjoyment from her next Warner short was her reunion with Pat O'Brien, who, together with his wife, had become one of her warm friends and supporters. They continued to laugh on set, as in their previous picture, and on weekends Davis and Ham went to the O'Briens for dinner.

The film in question, Bureau of Missing Persons, was filled with "calling-all-cars, follow-that-cab" situations, as one writer put it. It was set in a metropolitan police department's missing people division, where O'Brien was posted because he was too handy with his fists as a regular cop. Lewis Stone, his employer, believes he can calm down by tracing missing people in the department's "kindergarten."

Soon after, O'Brien becomes connected with a strange woman, played by Davis, who requests that he locate her missing husband, Alan Dinehart. She is later charged with her husband's death. She vanishes, and O'Brien reports that she has been discovered dead and will be buried at public expense. She appears at her own burial with Dinehart, who, it turns out, executed his mad twin brother. Davis, who had been found not guilty, and O'Brien rekindled their romantic desire, which they had only recently begun.

As the plot indicates, it was usually Warners keep-it-moving, keep-it-exciting stuff, and among its other issues, the Bureau of Missing Persons couldn't decide if it was a comedy, drama, melodrama, or a combination of all three.

Bureau was packed with good character actors for added insurance, including cynical, wisecracking Glenda Farrell as an ex-wife who drops in on a regular basis to ensure O'Brien's alimony payments to her, and addled-as-usual Hugh Herbert, a bureau employee who is perpetually preoccupied with finding a woman who, it turns out, works right in his office. (Ruth Donnelly performed this character well in one of her half-annoyed, half-wryly amused interpretations.)

In reality, the character actors were the finest thing about this mediocre film, which was based on a book, Missing Men, by John H. Ayers and Carol Bird. Davis was furious with photographer Barney McGill after seeing the finished product, who made her look like two separate people in mismatched photos. In several photos, she appeared nearly matronly—and she was only twenty-five!—while some appeared to be eighteen and fresh out of high school. Del Ruth paid her little attention, putting her to her own devices in terms of creativity. Given the rickety screenplay, the character actors stealing the scenes, and the fact that she only had a half-dozen sequences to portray, it's little surprise that a more than normally irritated Davis delivered one of her more strikingly uneven performances.

O'Brien did well in the film because his role followed the linear dramatic pattern of finding the perpetrator. In 1965, he told me about Davis's dissatisfaction with the film, her role, and the treatment she was receiving from the Warners.

"Ex-Lady, with her name above the title, had been her first official starring film and it flopped, through no fault of her own, and now, in Bureau of Missing Persons, she was back among the cast-not even 'first among equals' but, shall we say, 'equal among equals,' and it galled her no end," he stated. 'This photo is awful as hell,' she complained to me several times as I tried to coax her into a more relaxed mood on set. I remember her blowing up when some idiotic fan magazine published an item claiming that she and I were 'that way' about each other-even though we were both married and simply saw each other as friends! Oh, it all got to her-and I'm astonished, in retrospect, that it took her three years longer to leave the Warners!"

Interestingly, Davis could have entered the film industry as early as 1934, rather than having to wait until 1938 and Jezebel, because she was surprised and excited to learn that Emil Ludwig, the author of a much-praised and well-publicised biography of Napoleon, was negotiating with Jack Warner for the film rights. According to reports, he would even draft the screenplay with the assistance of one of the Warner hackers in order to give it "the requisite cinema interest."

The director, Robert Florey, was also involved in the talks, which consumed the first months of 1934. Ludwig and Florey were adamant that none other than Warners' "Little Giant," Edward G. Robinson, plays the Little Corporal, with Bette Davis leading the pack for the role of the empress Josephine, whom Napoleon eventually deserts for a more advantageous alliance with the Austrian archduchess Marie Louise, who gives him his heir.

George Arliss was similarly enthused about the idea, despite the fact that he had no involvement in it. He had expressed interest in playing Talleyrand, Napoleon's brilliant minister, but then changed his mind since he felt the character was not of starring calibre. During the filming of The Working Man, Davis discussed her desire to do a prestige costume drama with Arliss, and the sympathetic and concerned Arliss reportedly planted the idea of Davis as Josephine in the minds of Ludwig, Florey, and Warner, who expressed reservations about Davis in such a project.

"Is she up to costume stuff—I think of her as a modern girl," he hissed at Arliss and Florey, who instantly countered. The unwillingness of Edward G. Robinson to play Napoleon was the unexpected factor in all of these plots and alarums. Another case of a Warner star who would eventually excel in major customers (as would Davis) potentially delaying his "prestige period" for several years.

Robinson's motives for declining the part of Napoleon are unknown. Perhaps he was afraid his audience wouldn't accept him in the role, as Florey subsequently suggested, and opted to play it safe with gangsters and various mountebanks. Davis was devastated when the talks for Napoleon fell through, since she had been looking forward to playing alongside Robinson.

Napoleon, at least in his Hollywood incarnation (there had been a significant silent film covering elements of his life by Abel Gance), had to wait until Charles Boyer's superb performance in the 1937 MGM drama Conquest, alongside Greta Garbo as his mistress, Marie Walewska. (In that version, Josephine did not exist because she harkened back to a different time in the Little Corporal's life.)

Arliss attempted to soothe Davis by convincing Warner to lend her to another studio for his 1934 House of Rothschild, but Warner declined, citing the ingenue character as being too little and inappropriate to Davis's attitude.

In retrospect, Davis' loss of Josephine opposite Robinson's Napoleon may have been for the best, as the empress was not a particularly colourful or dynamic figure, and screenwriters who dealt with her (for example, the Merle Oberon impersonation in Marlon Brando's 1954 Désirée) never succeeded in fully bringing her to life.

However, prior to the release of Of Human Bondage in 1934, Davis was devastated by the loss of the role. And, within a few years, Jack Warner would be shown completely wrong regarding her appropriateness for costume parts.

It turned out that this was not the last time her wise tutor George Arliss tried to help her. His admiration for her remained undiminished. Meanwhile, Warners was determined to keep Davis firmly planted in Depression 1934, despite his wearing the most exquisite attire and performing beside the very 1934-ish William Powell.

The Davis-Powell chemistry did not work in Fashions of 1934, afterward known simply as Fashions, as I wrote in my Complete Films of William Powell. Powell is a "fashion pirate," constantly attempting to steal Parisian designs for cheaper sale in America. He and his aide, Davis, travel to the City of Light to engage in more piracy, with Frank McHugh accompanying them and sporting a hidden camera on the head of his cane. Hugh Herbert, who plays a California entrepreneur hoping to popularise the use of feathers on Paris gowns, provides a big portion of the laughs. All of this is accomplished with the assistance of phoney duchess Verree Teasdale, an old friend of Powell's from Hoboken, and crusty, snobbish fashion emperor Reginald Owen is brought to heel, culminating in an elaborate Busby Berkeley-choreographed fashion show, after which Powell and Davis return to America and, presumably, marriage.

"I had a lot of respect for Mr. Powell as an actor, but I wasn't particularly motivated to work with him again." "As much as I liked him, we just weren't right for each other in front of the camera, and I think the onscreen results prove it," Davis said years later.

Davis, according to director William Dieterle, was very much under Powell's shadow and disliked it. Furthermore, Perc Westmore and Orry-Kelly made sure she was dressed to the nines, with long, blond Garbo-esque hair, thick pancake makeup, the longest, falsest eyelashes they could produce, and slinky, over stylized clothes. "That kind of thing was for Harlow or Crawford—never for me," Davis later admitted. "In that picture I was frightfully ill at ease, and even felt embarrassed at times."

Davis was also irritated by having to watch some protracted comedy between Frank McHugh and Hugh Herbert in the back of a car, and as the scene plays now, she is clearly impatient and annoyed beneath her tight grin and forced attentiveness. "I've spent my entire life playing second fiddle—will it ever end?"" she inquired of producer Henry Blanke.

Powell, sensing her misgivings about him, kept his distance. That year, he was wrapping up his career at Warners before moving on to

MGM and even brighter success.

The New York Times' Mordaunt Hall commented, "The story is lively, the gowns are interesting, and the Busby Berkeley spectacles with Hollywood dancing girls are impressive." Instead of a conventional narrative about an enchantress who becomes an overnight queen of the Broadway stage, there is something distinctive in this picture." Another critic labelled Davis "letter-perfect," which she saw as a double-edged sword.

"I can't get out of these awful ruts," she told Photoplay editor Kathryn Dougherty at the time. They simply will not take me seriously. Look at me in this picture—I'm dressed like a third-rate impersonator of MGM glamour queens. That's not me. "I'll never be a clothes horse or romantic symbol," Dougherty said, implying that she had more potential in those areas than she realised, and that photographer William Rees had even made her look rather beautiful in certain pictures. "Beautiful never," Davis retorted. Striking occasionally, if I'm lucky!"

She still disliked seeing herself on film. "Everyone looks better than I do!""she bemoaned to Dieterle. "Verree Teasdale is more sophisticated and dresses better, Powell is centre stage in a flattering role, and McHugh and Herbert steal all the laughs." I merely stand there—as if I were an afterthought!"

Even the passionate addresses of Phillip Reed, who plays a songwriter in love with her, were insufficient solace. "He's cute, but too boyish for me," she said of the disappointed young Reed, who was one of many who "crushed" on her offscreen. Fashions was clearly a film she wanted to forget.

Davis was then hired opposite Charles Farrell, who had gained renown in the silent era as the leading male in Seventh Heaven opposite Janet Gaynor; they played a waifish couple languishing in a

Paris garret, and the world had embraced them. Farrell went on to do other films with Gaynor, and his career flourished with her and other co-stars into the talkie era, but by 1934, Farrell's career had plummeted, and The Big Shakedown, about a counterfeit drug racket, was a B picture and a "Big Comedown." Davis sensed his depression during the film and tried to comfort him as best she could. Although there was no romance, he did remember her warmth and understanding. "She's a gentler, sweeter, more understanding person than her publicity and reputation would lead one to believe," Charlie Farrell stated years later, after becoming the owner-manager of the Palm Springs Racquet Club and making a fortune. He then became mayor of Palm Springs and had a second career on television with My Little Margie and The Charlie Farrell Show. He was the husband of actress Virginia Valli for many years and was not a romantic wanderer.

"Charlie was a really sweet person," Davis said years later to Katherine Albert. "He was by no means a womaniser." He had more self-confidence than many men I've known in his macho, calm way, and didn't think he had to prove anything—and he didn't."

Katherine Albert also recalled Davis telling her that "Charlie was a real gentleman in his love scenes—never took advantage of the proximity to get fresh." She recalled Davis becoming irritated when she retorted that perhaps that was why the film came out so dull and second-rate—Charlie hadn't put enough moxie into his onscreen lovemaking!

Charlie is a druggist in The Big Shakedown, and Davis is his helpless wife. They become connected with a racketeer (Ricardo Cortez at his slimiest) who convinces Charlie to join a low-cost prescription-drug ring. When Farrell sees what is happening, he attempts to drop Cortez but is beaten and threatened. Farrell continues to go along with it because he is afraid Davis will be injured. Meanwhile, Davis's child dies as a result of a premature birth. Cortez is eventually killed by a business competitor, Henry O'Neill, and ends up in a vat of acid. The critic went on to say, "If only the acid had shown up earlier, it might have kept the audience from falling asleep."

The feedback was negative. "Far-fetched, over-acted, and unbelievable" was the most complimentary response. I was horrified when I saw the film many years later. John Francis Dillon's direction was sloppy to the extreme; he died soon after the film's completion, thus his worsening health could have had a role in the film's dismal performance. Sid Hickox did not give Davis the necessary photographic care; while she looks lovely, she lacks the delicate lighting that emphasises her actual uniqueness as it was evolving by early 1934. Niven Busch and Rain James' screenplay is jumbled and lacks cumulative impact, while the editing is abrupt and flimsy.

"I was in that film, and Bette's unhappiness with it was a depressing thing to watch," character actor Allen Jenkins told me many years later. We'd drink coffee every now and again. She was very democratic with her crew and co-stars, and I recall her stating that Glenda Farrell had the meaty part as a shady lady, and she'd rather have two minutes on screen in a character with bite than an hour and a half simpering and cooing, as she did in this. I didn't blame her for being a jerk about it all."

Davis and Jimmy Cagney, Warners' other stormy-petrel rebel, had become friends, and they were thrilled to be cast together in Jimmy the Gent (formerly Always a Gent), based on an original story, The Heir Chaser, by Laird Doyle and Ray Nazarro, who wrote it with Jimmy—and no one else—in mind. Jimmy had just returned from one of his numerous Warner suspensions, and he described Gent as "crapola—but slightly better-class crapola than usual." Davis, who adored Jimmy and thought he was one of the best actors in Hollywood, had lamented over the years that they had not gotten a better vehicle in which to play; they later did another, with equally unfavourable results.

Jimmy the Gent tells the story of an opportunist (Cagney) who specialises in finding heirs to lost properties and then sharing in the take. Davis, Jimmy's secretary-girlfriend, despises Jimmy's shady business activities and abandons him, siding with his business adversary, Alan Dinehart, whom she regards as honest, upright, conservative, and a gentleman.

Jimmy then sets out to imitate Dinehart, refining his speech, dressing more conservatively, hosting "tea parties" for his cup staff, and so on. Davis is unimpressed, so Jimmy decides to expose Dinehart for the scumbag that he is, with predictable results.

The film ran a typical 66 minutes for a 1934 Warner product, and Michael Curtiz directed at his usual frantic, slam-bang pace, which emerged on the screen as fast, furious, riveting, and highly entertaining to fans who lapped up fast action stuff with no regard for quality dramatics, which Jimmy the Gent lacked.

Jimmy Cagney had a strong connection with Davis, whom he saw as a fellow quality seeker. He was in a better position to offer the obstinate Warner executives what they deserved at the time because he was paid more than Davis and his box-office clout was formidable.

Jimmy, a gritty Manhattan street kid, had climbed up in vaudeville and achieved success on Broadway, always doing things the hard way, and he was more than a match for the Warners. He was the quintessential Depression-era hero, not only as a mobster but also in numerous versions of the spunky, industrious common man buffeted by fate who always lands on his feet, foursquare. In 1961, he told me about Davis:

"You know, Bette came from old Yankee stock, from a pretty patrician family, but she was a fighter!" Working with her in Jimmy the Gent was like baking in a hot oven—it was hot and stuffy, but you couldn't wait to see how the cake ended! She was a fantastic talent, and I don't know how she put up with all those second-rate parts—some of them a cut above bits—that they imposed on her for years. I believe that was the Warners' way of punishing her for her rash complaints, but she was such a trooper that she delivered on every assignment, no matter how bad the lines and settings were. I was fortunate in that I was a lead, and then a star, from almost the start, so I understood her frustration more than others. She turned on the current as soon as she came on stage and never turned it off. That woman's vigour! Words cannot express how I feel."

Cagney, like Davis, lamented the fact that neither had a strong vehicle to do together, with the two they did being clearly second- and third-rate.

"Jimmy had a vitality that matched my own, and he had wonderfully unpredictable little twists and catches and surprises in his technique that kept me on my toes," Davis observed at the time. "What a delight he was to play with!" There was no placidity, artificial hauteur, or phoney composure about him! He was always very much himself, so real, so true—wish I'd had more Jimmy Cagneys to play with!"

Bette Davis seemed to value Fog Over Frisco more than some of the other Warner projects she was working on at the time. "I loved my part, William Dieterle directed me expertly, I looked fine, and I was very pleased with the film," she said Katherine Albert, a fan magazine writer. Davis's reaction to Fog Over Frisco is perplexing in retrospect, because when I watched it years later, I considered it to be conventional Warners melodrama at breakneck speed. The film is completely unremarkable, and Davis is barely visible; Margaret Lindsay and Donald Woods, purportedly her supporters, get more screen time.

Davis is a wild society girl with an obvious death wish who enjoys illegal bond dealings with an underworld monarch (Irving Pichel) who owns a nightclub. Lindsay, her stepsister, decides to investigate how deeply Davis is connected. The Davis character appears to have included her fiancé, Lyle Talbot, in her deeds. When the nightclub owner discovers she has attempted to betray him, he murders her, kidnaps Lindsay, and eventually gets his comeuppance.

This is the plot of Fog Over Frisco, and as previously stated, there is nothing that distinguishes it from a dozen other Warner products of its type. Davis' positive reaction to the picture may have been affected by Tony Gaudio's beautiful photographs of her and her fashionable wardrobe, but the screenplay by Robert N. Lee and Eugene Solow, based on George Dyer's original story, appears to be unworthy of Dieterle's clearly endless efforts. Margaret Lindsay and Donald Woods do well in the end, and when told thirty years later that Davis thought Fog Over Frisco was quite good, Lindsay, too, expressed surprise. She stated:

"I never understood why she took such a small part-she just wasn't in evidence that much-and while I know she liked to play bad girls, this particular girl was not all that interesting in my opinion." I enjoyed my part and was surprised that I had more to do than Bette, but I don't consider it a watershed moment for myself, her, or anyone else involved!"

At the time, critics agreed with Lindsay rather than Davis. "A veneer of theatricalism prevails throughout," Variety wrote. "The story, in the way it's brought to the screen, never quite strikes a convincing note," according to Mordaunt Hall of The New York Times.

William Dieterle never thought much of the film, claiming it was one of a series of trifling potboilers imposed on him by the studio during "that unfortunate era" before he eventually got the "big" Warner topics he deserved.

Even in drek, Dieterle could be a martinet in a European style that irritated Davis as much as Curtiz's more crude, frequently scatological approach. This did not prevent her from working successfully with him later, during his "big" era.

Davis was described by Lyle Talbot in 1960 as being "lost in a trance" while studying her script and practising nuances of her voice and inflections "as if she had been handed a Shaw or Shakespeare assignment." Her unwavering focus was unsettling. Her self-involvement struck me as a type of selfishness-true, she worked well with the other players and the crew, but I always got the impression she was just concerned with herself and the effect she was generating." Significantly, Talbot continued, "I always felt she must be a tough woman to be married to."

7.

Of Human Bondage-and Recognition

THE IMAGE THAT WAS TO TRANSFORM DAVIS'S LIFE AND CAREER WAS ON THE verge of not happening. In early 1934, Jack Warner flatly refused to cast her as Mildred, the slatternly, vicious waitress in RKO's adaptation of Somerset Maugham's novel Of Human Bondage. For six months, she pleaded with him for the money; she remembered showing up at his office every morning "with the shoeshine boy." Meanwhile, she remained on the Warner chain gang, playing poor roles in execrable, shoddy, second-rate films. She wandered sullenly from set to set, doing her job, desperately searching for anything in the cardboard characters and screenplays that she could develop into something real and human.

Finally, in the spring of 1934, two events occurred that tipped the scales in her favour. Jack Warner requested that RKO lend him Irene Dunne for the musical Sweet Adeline. Human Bondage director John Cromwell encouraged producer Pandro Berman to offer Jack an exchange: Davis for Dunne. The second element was Jack Warner's hesitant but yet admiring reaction to Davis's nasty, murdering Marie Roark in Bordertown rushes. He informed his colleagues that he thought Davis could handle Mildred and that, while it was a risk, if she did well in the part, she would be more important to the studio—and Bordertown would be more valuable as well. He called her in and told her the loanout had been arranged, much to her delight. "The role may hurt you—the public may recoil from Mildred, associate her with you, and back off from you—but go and hang yourself if you must!" he snarled. He wisely delayed the release of Bordertown for six months.

The first filmmaker to cast Davis in a large, blockbuster role was John Cromwell. He had extensive Broadway experience before coming to films in 1928 as an actor, director, and producer, but gradually specialised in directing and by 1934 had established a solid reputation as a fine technician and sensitive director of actors, as in Lionel Barrymore's Sweepings (1933) and Irene Dunne's The Silver Cord (1934). He had noticed Davis's remarkable magnetism in Cabin in the Cotton and Ex-Lady, among other films, and thought she would be perfect for Mildred and have the bravery to play her without restraint or punch-pulling. Again, George Arliss worked behind the scenes to secure the project for her, arranging for his friend Somerset Maugham to inspect the work done by Davis and Arliss via prints shipped to England. Maugham gave Davis his unequivocal approval as Mildred.

Maugham didn't merely go out of his way to delight his friend Arliss or to give the ambitious young lady at Warners a chance. Of Human Bondage was a novel as dear to him as David Copperfield had been to Charles Dickens in a very different setting. Both had done a lot of autobiographical soul-searching for their novels. Maugham, who had a speech impediment since childhood, had made his character, Philip, a club-footed cripple. Like Philip, he had suffered the humiliations of unrequited love for an unworthy object—in Maugham's case, another man—more than once. This recall of his own life gives Of Human Bondage the painful reality and sincerity that garnered it a devoted following.

Lester Cohen, the film's screenwriter, made the reproduction of Maugham's autobiographical suffering as accurate and authentic as the drastically different cinematic medium allowed. Given that he had only 83 minutes to convey all of the complexity of Maugham's deeply felt novel, Cohen's script is commendable workmanlike.

Maugham's barely veiled alter ego, Philip Carey, has abandoned painting in Paris to study medicine in London; if destined to be a second- or third-rate artist, he is resolved to become a first-rate doctor. He meets Mildred Rogers, a sluttily lovely but ignorant and rude server, in a tearoom. He becomes obsessed with her. He pursues her despite her terrible character flaws and sadistic flirtatiousness, despite the fact that she makes no bones about finding his handicapped state repulsive and rebuffs his love overtures. During the course of the action, she kills him for two men: a smarmy salesman who abandons her when she is pregnant, and a more gorgeous medical student with whom she flees. Meanwhile, two warmly compassionate young women develop feelings for Philip, but he is too hurt and distracted by Mildred to react. Furthermore, his self-image has been so wounded that he is unable to perceive that their romantic interest in him is genuine.

Philip, who is still masochistically attached to Mildred, takes her in when she is in need, and when he rebuffs the physical advances she makes as a sort of payment for his kindness, recognizing that there is no affection or true commitment in them, she taunts him for his deformities, destroys his apartment, including the bonds that are putting him through medical school, and disappears yet again.

Then two wonderful things happen to Philip. He obtains an inheritance that secures his future as a doctor, and he begins a healthy relationship with a lovely young lady. Mildred, on the other hand, has not been forgotten. He discovers she is dying from tuberculosis in a charity unit. Her death liberates him from his attachment, allowing him to resume his true life, both personally and professionally.

Such is scriptwriter Cohen's distilled cinematic version of Maugham's work, which, to Cohen's credit, captures all of the psychological essence of what Maugham was attempting to express about the human bondage of unrequited infatuation for an undesirable object.

In 1968, at the age of 79, John Cromwell told me what he saw in a twenty-six-year-old Bette Davis that made him as eager to cast her as Mildred as she was to portray her. "Mildred was a role that many actresses of the day avoided out of fear. She was a slatternly sadist, unsympathetic to the extreme, and her dress, postures, and overall appearance were all seedy, miserable, and sleazy in a way that no nineteen-four glamour lady would ever dare to mimic. Bette Davis couldn't care less about any of it! "There was an actress under all that phoney overlay and she knew it and I knew it and, to his credit, my producer, Pandro Berman knew it." She wanted to give honest characterizations—unadorned, brutally true and honest, if possible—and at Warners they were dolling her up in blond wigs and fancy clothes and drowning her in glitz and schmaltz and gangster-action stuff and all the rest of it. Maugham felt the same way. "George Arliss felt the same way."

Davis, who was unhappy in her marriage and dissatisfied and irritated with her little roles at Warners, attacked Mildred with a ferocity that astounded her coworkers. It eventually astounded the film's lead, Leslie Howard. Howard, a famous Broadway star in 1934, had appeared with such cinematic first ladies as Norma Shearer and Mary Pickford, and had travelled first class all the way. The ethereal, poetic-looking Howard had done some hard living by 1934, when he was forty, but looked ten years younger, Dorian Gray style, as a compulsive womaniser and disloyal to his long-suffering wife. Davis' posting to Bondage had not pleased him. This small blond child, not particularly attractive or sexually enticing (at least to his taste), appeared to be an afterthought.

Howard acted patronisingly while reading novels, feeding her line readings almost as an afterthought. Then he noticed the rushes. Howard was startled to learn he was working with a first-rate actress, a vibrant original unlike anybody he had ever met. His weary indifference turned to intense intensity. Howard, a male prima donna driven by professional jealousy, began to play back to her as one demanding scenario followed another. In some of them, he was supposed to reply to her harsh, vulgar excoriations with white-faced, cowering horror. What Howard didn't realise (or perhaps he did, being a consummate professional) was that by meeting her halfway, listening, reacting, and playing back to her on her level, he was boosting Davis's performance.

Davis' ego was stung by Howard's lack of sexual interest in her offscreen. She reasoned that if the English Adonis didn't want her sexually, she would whip him into respecting her professionally if he thought she was just another conveyer-belt blonde nothing from the Warner sausage factory. She was successful with her second goal.

Howard was prejudiced toward her at first because she was American. With so many beautiful English actresses to choose from, he asked Cromwell and Berman what made her so exceptional. What's the big deal about bringing this unremarkable monster over from Warners? They corrected him on these issues. No English actress would take on such an unattractive role. And Davis, a true

New England Yankee, was of English ancestry. And she'd hired a Cockney servant, who stayed with her for eight weeks while Davis mastered the nuances—she drove Ham insane by speaking in a Cockney accent even in bed.

But after experiencing these rushes, Howard didn't need any more sales pitches.

Later in Of Human Bondage, there is a sequence that has gone down in film history. Davis, outraged by Howard's rejection of her crude physical approaches, insults him viciously. It's worth repeating the chat (on her side), complete with her Cockney accent: *"Yew cad, yew dirty swine! I never cared for yew-not once! I was always making a fool of yuh! Yuh bored me stiff! I hated yuh! It made me sick when I had to let yuh kiss me! I only did it because yuh begged me. Yuh hounded me, yuh drove me crazy, and after yuh kissed me, I always used to wipe my mouth! Wipe my mouth! But I made up for it. For every kiss I had to laugh! We laughed at yuh! Miller and me! Griffith and me! We laughed at yuh because yuh were such a mug, a mug, a mug! You know what you are, you gimpy-legged monster? You're a cripple, a cripple, a cripple!"*

Davis painted a portrait of concentrated feminine viciousness so stunning and electrically venomous that it stunned spectators. She was brave as an artist in refusing to give Mildred any redeeming characteristics, any fake Hollywood audience sympathy. Mildred was a natural force, lightning-like, a monster of hatred and malevolence. Davis recognized that mature, receptive, sensitive audiences would detect the underlying bitterness, deprivation, and kicking around Mildred had suffered from a series of men, all of which had given her a scorn for the human species.

Davis conveys Mildred's fatigue from being on her feet all day, her bone-tiredness, and her cynical scepticism of any guy who smiles at her when Philip first meets her. When confronted with the poetic, sensitive cripple, she is at a loss for words. Her brutalised personality then detects that this is a man who is sweet on her, making her vulnerable and pliable. Here's a man she can dominate, mistreat, and humiliate, and he'll return for more. Above all, Davis' Mildred finds in Howard's Philip someone she can repay, as a vulnerable, love-castrated emblem of the male sex, for all the mistreatment she has endured from men her entire life as a result of her poverty, her bottom-step caste. He is someone to take advantage of and use. She cannot see his love as genuine because he is unlike any other man she has encountered. Mildred Davis sees male softness as weakness; sensitivity as effeminate; and decency as tame.

Many people have puzzled how Davis was able to portray Mildred so realistically. They reasoned that her life had always been safe: she had the security of a contract while others starved in the depths of the Depression; she had a mother who had shielded her from the harsher realities at every turn; and she was safely married, after twenty-four years of prim virginity, to a "nice young man" who seemed harmless. What they didn't see was the enormous reservoir of anger Davis had built up over the years: anger at her father, who had abandoned her; anger at the poverty that had forced her mother to work so hard; anger at the Warner overlords who had frustrated her best career instincts; and, the year she made Of Human Bondage, anger at her husband and her mother, who had forced her to abort two babies "so as not to deflect your career energies, Bette."

She also drew on her sense-memory—of the hours she had spent at school as a waitress to earn money, of her envy of girls who had generous allowances and a caring mother and father. And, just as Mildred had Philip pay for all the humiliations inflicted on her by men, Davis made Howard pay for the deserting father, the tyrant studio master, the weak husband who had failed in his conventional position.

All of this culminated in a performance that debuted on June 28, 1934, at Radio City Music Hall to critical acclaim and audience shock—shock that quickly evolved into a half-horrified, half-admiring awareness of an exciting new star, one of an entirely different order and makeup—an authentic original.

Davis remembers Ham and Ruthie's responses when they returned home after witnessing a preview of the film. They entered the house in startled silence, she recounted, and when she asked them for their reaction, they said the job would either make or ruin her.

They didn't have to wait long for an answer.

The critics went overboard with superlatives. They noticed that she didn't care about her appearance; her clothing was dirty and ripped; her makeup was sloppy, making her look like a cheap slacker; and her walk was a dejected slouch.

A moment near the end of the film, when Philip discovers her in the final stages of tuberculosis, is one of the most striking examples of Davis' uncompromising realism. In one scenario, she appears so terrifying that youngsters and sensitive adults in the audience hide behind their seats. Her eyes are profoundly veiled, her face is grey and pale, and her mouth is contorted by disease and pain, hatred, malice, and frustration. It has the appearance of corruption and decomposition, as well as a partially decomposed corpse. Only Davis would have dared to appear like that in 1934, when everything was glamour-silly and traditional. Only a genius could have pulled it off. That she did.

Some detractors missed the meaning and accused her of exaggerating Mildred. "When it came to these final, ultimate, crucial scenes, I let Bette have her head; I trusted her instincts," John Cromwell told me. A director can assist, but the artist must unearth the truth within herself. And that is what Better provided us in Of Human Bondage: the truth, which in actuality is frequently exactly that—a harsh, horrible exaggeration. Hasn't it been said that life is weirder than fiction—and even more exaggerated? That's exactly what Bette offered us in that picture!"

"It is perhaps the best performance ever recorded on the screen by a U.S. actress," Life remarked of Davis's Mildred. "Few people realised that she had the ability to understand and interpret the role so successfully," Film Weekly stated.

The New York Times' Mordaunt Hall topped all other critical aces, noting, "An enormously effective portrayal is that of Bette Davis as Mildred Rogers." ...The audience was so enraged by this vixen's behaviour at the first [Radio City Music Hall] showing of this picture yesterday that when Carey finally expressed his contempt for Mildred's behaviour, applause erupted from all sides." Hall licked his chops over the "climactic episode, which recalls an incident in Kipling's The Light That Failed." Carey's artistic attempts are slashed, his medical books and furniture are destroyed, and his bonds and private files are burned, leaving the apartment as if it had been hit by a storm!"

If Davis had anticipated to be treated like Ruth Chatterton at Warners, she was quickly disappointed. Back to the salt mines and the drek, back to her rage and anguish. Later, when she was mentioned for an Academy Award nomination, Warners instructed their employees to vote for other actresses—her smash was made outside the home lot, so why should RKO get any breaks? Davis was left out of the three 1934 nominations, which went to Norma Shearer in The Barretts of Wimpole Street, Grace Moore in One Night of Love, and Claudette Colbert in It Happened One Night. (Many years later, Davis would triumph in a job that Colbert had dropped out of due to an accident; fate, ever unexpected and quixotic, made amends.)

The public outpouring of rage at Davis's snub prompted the launch of a write-in campaign for her. As a result of missing out, Davis received more recognition for what many thought to be the best actress's performance in 1934 than Colbert did as the eventual winner. This culminated in Davis receiving the first of a succession of legendary "consolation prizes"—an Oscar for a performance in a previous year's film that had somehow gone unnoticed. In addition, the Academy regulations were altered to provide for a more real representation of the industry's will during Oscar season, with Price-Waterhouse tasked to ensure correct and authentic vote tabulations.

There has been great controversy over whether Bette Davis named the Academy Award "Oscar" because the trophy resembled Ham's backside, whose middle name was Oscar.

During the course of researching this book, a little-known truth that deserves additional investigation emerged—an instance that does not appear in earlier publications on Bette Davis. Kirtley Baskette noted in the May 1935 Photoplay magazine piece, "The Girl They Tried to Forget," that "Hollywood championed [Davis] so vigorously [for the 1934 award] that for a while the whole town seemed to be one giant indignation meeting." Editorials, articles, telegrams, and phone calls deluged the austere Academy until, like the befuddled author in Once in a Lifetime, its members concluded that "it couldn't all be a typographical error." Baskette's postman, he wrote, thought the Academy's slight was "a darn outrage," and that Baskette should "give 'em the devil!""The little-known fact was Baskette's statement that by the spring of 1935, the Academy had handed Davis a "belated" honour, a "special commendation." If this is true, Davis must have kept this acknowledgment secretly stowed away somewhere.

Back at Warners from RKO, Davis was handed another "sausage." Housewife was a film that Davis despised before, during, and after she appeared in it, and for many years afterwards she, along with director Alfred Green and screenwriters Robert Lord and Lillie Hayward, took the name Housewife in vain. Her dissatisfaction could also be attributed to the fact that Orry-Kelly, who is usually dependable, must have been on mental leave when he designed her costumes for this, and that a cameraman with whom she rarely worked, William Rees, lit her rather poorly, causing her eyes to bulge and her jaw to stick out more sternly than usual.

In The New York Times, Frank S. Nugent confirmed her opinion of the hapless Housewife, enraging her with observations such as:

"One of the characteristics of a bad boxer is that he telegraphs his punches." The dramatic blows in Housewife are not only telegraphed, but radioed. The most perplexing aspect of the picture is the startling frequency with which the unexpected fails to occur. ...Mr. Brent and Miss Dvorak perform admirably, although Miss Davis is a little too blatant as the siren."

Housewife, which I reread fifty years later, is every bit the shambles everyone claimed it was. It's a grab bag of every 1934 Warner cliché imaginable. Brent, the errant husband, neglects his wife (Dvorak) in favour of a stunning ex-girlfriend (Davis). The husband gets his comeuppance when he injures his little son and ends up in the hospital. After considerable tension, the boy is found to be well. Wife is upset because she contributed to her husband's prosperity, and now he is out on the town with swinger Davis. She exacts her vengeance by visiting one of her husband's clients, John Halliday. Finally, the husband learns that the success of his ad agency is attributable to his wife. All of the main characters wind up in court, where the husband sees the light. Back to the small woman, exit siren, and so on.

Davis throws it on thick as the would-be home wrecker, behaving with more reckless obviousness than usual (one wonders where director Alfred Green was during her seemingly self-directed excesses). Brent and Dvorak seem generally on top of things, but as the fourth member of the romance ring, the seasoned character actor John Halliday steals whatever there is to steal.

The year Housewife was produced, George Brent's marriage to Ruth

Chatterton fell apart, and Davis seemed to be living offscreen her position as home-breaking siren now that George was set to join the armies of the free. In actuality, she did not end the marriage, and Chatterton was far from a typical housewife!

According to Alfred Green, Brent was easing out of the Chatterton marriage as gracefully as possible during Housewife, and while he continued having affairs with unknowns who could be kept at a distance, the upfront spectacle of co-star Davis following him back to his dressing room and manoeuvring herself next to him for lunch in the commissary unnerved him somewhat—especially given Ham Nelson's reputation for temper tantrums. Davis stated it took her until the late 1930s to pique Brent's interest in her, thus her dissatisfaction with his lack of response during the filming of the ill-fated Housewife must have caused her psychic overload.

Bordertown, the film Davis made soon before Of Human Bondage, was finally released in January 1935 by Jack Warner.

Bordertown stands out amid the regular Davis-Warner offerings of the time because it allows her to perform. It is the film that convinced Jack Warner, once and for all, to cast Davis as Mildred in Of Human Bondage, because he and his executives were so impressed with her performance as Marie Roark, the cheap-minded, sluttish, sex-deprived wife of a fat, messy casino owner in a Mexican border town.

It's unclear why Bordertown wasn't released until six months following Of Human Bondage, which premiered in June 1934. According to director Archie Mayo, Jack Warner intuitively recognized Bondage would return Davis to his studio as a more important star, and Bordertown, in which she also had a strong role, would produce a respectable follow-up (despite the terrible Housewife that came between).

Bordertown is truly Paul Muni's picture, as it realistically portrays him as an ambitious Mexican-American who accepts a position in Eugene Pallette's casino-night spot after experiencing racial discrimination and derision in his law business. He assists Pallette in making the company a success, then scornfully rejects Paulette's wife, Davis, when she sets her sights on him. Davis lets the garage door close on her intoxicated husband, asphyxiating him with carbon monoxide fumes in a famous and, at the time, unusually designed murder scene. She later falsely accuses Muni of murder because she is envious of his attention to society girl Margaret Lindsay.

Davis chose to depict growing mental illness on the witness stand at this moment by using minor eye movements and facial tension. Archie Mayo, who liked his melodrama hot and hollery, and Jack Warner clashed with her about it. They wanted her to go full-on crazy and chew the scenery, believing that was what viewers expected of a "loony," but Davis challenged them to let the scene stand at a theatre preview; if the audience didn't like it, she'd retake it. The scene survived because the audience enjoyed it.

When viewed many years later, the scene appears short and insufficient. Davis is given insufficient conversation and business to be effective, which is partly down to Mayo and the screenwriters, Lillie Hayward and Manuel Seff. It seems to end abruptly, with no natural progression or development. A hybrid of the two approaches would have been the most beneficial.

Davis gets over all the frenzied viciousness that makes her so remarkable in the earlier scenes, when she strides around, frantic with irritation over Muni's unresponsiveness, snarky to her dumb servant, outraged over his cold contempt when he realises she has literally killed for him. If Jack Warner was so impressed with her after seeing Bordertown that he allowed her to go to RKO for Bondage, then why would he dump her back into gutless drek for the next two years, with a few exceptions?

Davis's first collaboration with Paul Muni, a great performer with exquisite ego and power. He was a Yiddish theatrical performer who subsequently found success on Broadway. Muni meticulously prepared for his roles, never hesitating to modify his appearance and mentality in order to create an authentic character. Muni was trying to convey the frustrations and strivings of an ambitious Mexican-American wanting to rise beyond his beginnings and make his people proud. He was painstaking, thorough, and filled with the talent that best expresses itself by taking infinite pains.

It irritated him to be pitted against Davis, an artist of a different calibre who was hell-bent on impressing her vivid personality and frenzied passion on her characters. Muni despised the rivalry because he felt he had found his match. Worse, her vivid interpretation compelled him to play second fiddle. He promised Warner that he would never work with her again. "She's too hoggy, too egocentric, she doesn't stay within the framework of her role," Warner said, seeing through his envy and insecurities. "I'm serious—no more pictures with Davis!"" Muni exclaimed. It would be five years before their names appeared together above a film's title, and by then, both had risen to the pinnacle of celebrity. But they didn't appear in a single scene together!

Meanwhile, the film was playing all over the country in January 1935, and Muni and his supportive, sustaining wife, Bella, simmered and seethed over such rave reviews as The New York Times' Andre Sennwald, who wrote, "[Davis] plays the part with the ugly, sadistic, and utterly convincing sense of reality which distinguished her fine performance in Of Human Bondage."

Bella Muni devised her husband's response to this. He approached Jack Warner and requested more money and greater positions. His overcompensatory determination in the face of Davis's "threat" earned him an Academy Award within two years.

Davis was billed above the title for The Girl From 10th Avenue after the success of Bordertown and the many accolades she received for her work in it convinced Warners that she was ready for the "star treatment." The gesture was premature for the second time because the 69-minute vehicle brought out to back her regained "status" wasn't up to the fine and earnest acting she put into every frame.

This time, she's a girl from New York's 10th Avenue who runs into a social lawyer, Ian Hunter, as he's preparing to make a scene outside the church where his ex-fiancée (Katherine Alexander) is marrying another guy (Colin Clive). Several narrative twists later, Davis marries him on the rebound, they live in her apartment, and she is learning proper manners with the help of her ex-Floradora Girl landlord, Alison Skipworth, in preparation for her transfer to Park Avenue.

But when fickle Miss Alexander tries to entice Hunter back by highlighting her marriage to Clive as a mistake, Davis chooses to fight for him since she has fallen in love. Clive finally persuades Hunter to stay with his wife Davis at the end of the film.

Davis's starring roles in The Girl From 10th Avenue were both interesting. Ian Hunter was a gorgeous, if reserved, British actor who had served in World War I, risen through the ranks of the London stage, and then moved to Hollywood. He specialised in dancing for the many love troubles of soap tragedies like Kay Francis, and while Davis liked him and worked with him in future films, she found him too tame for her tastes and failed to reciprocate his obvious interest, much to his sorrow. Hunter handled his rejection with civility, which could not be said for the other man on 10th Avenue, Colin Clive, who developed a neurotic rather than real interest in her. Davis found it more difficult to refuse his approaches. Clive, a former English theatre actor, had a smash with Journey's End during World War I, but was quickly confined to starkly unwholesome characters in films like Frankenstein and Mad Love. He played the scientist who conjures up the monster in the first film, and the wild-eyed pianist who is given the hands of a murderer after his own are injured and amputated in the second. Clive fitted roles like these considerably better than frothy romances. He was attractive, but his tense, on-edge demeanour made the women in the crowd apprehensive. He died of drunkenness in 1937, like another brother-under-the-skin, Monroe Owsley. He was a tortured and confused bisexual who suffered humiliating gay outbursts that left him dejected, and as Ian Hunter later recounted, "Colin was a wonderful actor but he made everyone around him nervous—nervous as hell! One didn't want to be in the neighbourhood of what appeared to be an impending blow up, breakdown, or both."

During breaks on the film, while Hunter provided genteel English tea sessions for Davis, Clive, as director Alfred Green recounted, would wander off to a far, gloomy corner and brood and glower. In later years, Davis stated that she found Clive captivating if physically ugly, at least to her, and he certainly matched her passion on screen, "though his," as she put it, "was an altogether different ballgame." Offscreen, his advances left her feeling "creepy."

She later regretted not having Clive as her main starring man—in 10th Avenue, he was more of a supporting character, and their onscreen clashes were minimal. Green remembered her remarking that very few male performers could equal her intensity. If some people considered her a witch, Clive was a warlock, and their onscreen chemistry would have been fantastic.

Of course, Davis was preoccupied with George Brent at the time, but she discussed both Hunter and Clive with Brent and Al Green. According to Al Green, Brent thought both men to be funny and completely inappropriate as suitors, snickering, "One [Hunter] is a milksop who'd bore you to death and the other is a maniac who might cut your head off some night and plunk it on the icebox!'" Instead of shuddering in horror at such direct language, Davis threw her head back and laughed hysterically," Green stated. "How do you know I wouldn't cut off his head?'" she responded. Clive did another Frankenstein film for Universal the following year. In this one, The Bride of Frankenstein, he creates a monster woman (Elsa Lanchester was a hit in the role) as a wife for his original monster, and Brent and Green jokingly told Davis that if she'd only successfully pleaded with Jack Warner for a loan out on that, she and Clive could have raised old Satan himself!

Charles Kenyon, the scriptwriter for The Girl From 10th Avenue, customised the principal character to Davis's full measure. As soapy and frivolous as the image was, it depicted her as a daring lower-class dame raising herself to the social level where she could compete on equal terms with her adversary and win her upper-class guy via sheer nerve and earnest address. She certainly had plenty of opportunities here to march purposefully about, flash her eyes kinetically, and deliver the brash, combative statements that had become her trademark by then. Hunter, who was more docile, but sophisticated, was the perfect counterbalance for all of this.

The New York Times praised Davis' portrayal as "both truthful and amusing," while Variety praised her for going "high, wide, and handsome on the emotions."

8.

Grinding out the Warner Sausage

IN MID-1935, while she was stuck in one of her Warner horrors, Front Page Woman, Davis said:

"At this time, the Warners were perplexed by me. I did my job-and did it well—regardless of what crap they assigned me to do or how much I scornfully sniffed at it. If they refused to assist me, I would assist myself. Critics and the public were elevating me, but they resisted.

"My graduating contract appeared to the studio to be adequate compensation for my work, but money was not an issue." They were all used to actors who were grateful to have been rescued from diners or from beneath damp stones and were content as long as the money came in. Everything was well with their universe as long as their paychecks weren't timid and their billing was bold."

During this time, she felt she was being treated "as an intractable child." She recalled meeting Jack Warner at parties, where he would patronise her maddeningly, wagging his finger at her like a disapproving parent, using irritating variations on: "Remember, Bette, you have to be at the studio at six o'clock." Get some rest soon!"

This usually irritated her because she was known on set for her promptness and disliked being treated like a five-year-old.

More notable is a mention in her biography of Jack Warner's lack of adulterous tendencies. "In all fairness," she added, "he was unique as a film mogul." He was not a lecherous employer! His crimes were hidden elsewhere. He was the son's father. The authority. The honour. And he was in business to profit. I was aware of this, but I was and still am convinced that if good work is offered in the same packaging as trash, the public will buy it."

Katherine Albert informed me that Davis was irritated by Jack Warner's virtue, at least in her opinion. "God, the man must wear an iron chastity belt," Katherine snarled. Davis, according to the same source, began making unnecessary visits to Warner's office in an attempt to attract him. "I just want to check to see if he's human," she joked. She once caught Jack without his pants because he was getting measured for a new suit in his office and didn't have time to hurry down to his preferred tailor.

"Jack, your legs are fantastic," she said admiringly.

"Bette, hurry up and leave!"" he responded. His aide quickly showed her the way out.

Davis, still stung by Laemmle's remark that she had "as much sex appeal as Slim Summerville," was anxious to stir Warner. Katherine cautioned her that she was violating the moral-turpitude clause in her contract, which was required by the Production Code and the Legion of Decency, which dominated Hollywood in 1935, but Davis claimed she didn't care.

"People are flouting it all the time—look at the way Darryl Zanuck acts," Davis declared defiantly, but she eventually stopped "trying to get into the boss's pants," as producer Henry Blanke put it, because she grew fond of Warner's wife, Ann, who always treated her graciously. Ann Warner would eventually become an important Davis ally, so her foresight in bringing in her seduction horns may have been instinctual. There was also the obvious reality that Jack Warner had no sexual interest in Bette Davis.

Jerry Asher, a writer who knew Davis well, felt this bothered her. "She became quite vain about her alleged ability to get any man she wanted," Jerry said. "First it was George Brent, and now it's the Grand Panjandrum himself!""

Jerry also believed that her many squabbles with Jack Warner over the years stemmed not only from her ambition to achieve a superb product, but also from hurt vanity, which Davis vehemently denied.

Brent had been legally free of Ruth Chatterton for a year by 1935 and was available for grabbing—at the bodies of several attractive

Hollywood women, some actresses, some even married, which made Warner extremely nervous, given those eternal moral-turpitude clauses. According to Henry Blanke, Jack summoned George to his office one day. "Why don't you get married again, George?"" he started.

"No thanks-like my liberty!"" (Brent was known for his succinct responses.)

"All right, why don't you give Davis a tumble!" She's had feelings for you for years!"

"She's a married woman, Jack."

"When has that ever stopped you? Anyway, I'm going to place you two in another image. In fact, two in a row. The public enjoys seeing you together. They are aware of the sexual tension. On Screen, it comes across as genuine."

"Perhaps from her. No, not from me."

"You begin shooting on Monday at seven o'clock. Get out now!"

"Glad to."

Front Page Woman, the first of two 1935 films co-starring Bette Davis and George Brent, depicts Brent falling in love with Davis despite his belief that she is a "bum newspaperwoman." "All women are bums in such a job," observes ace reporter Brent on a regular basis. He dupes Davis into reporting an incorrect murder verdict due to his machinations, and she is dismissed as a result. Then she is compelled to restore the balance, which she does for the rest of the fast-paced but unexpectedly uninteresting and perfunctory events.

Fans were drawn to Davis's wide-eyed stares at Brent throughout the scenes in which they were together. Davis made the mistake of taking Ham Nelson to see Front Page Woman, and Mike Curtiz recalls them fighting along the lines of:

"You must be in love with that guy the way you ogle him constantly in front of the camera."

"But Ham, I'm paid to be an actress and you have to look interested in your leading man."

"Horseshit!"

The proceedings, based on ex-newspaperman Richard Macauley's story "Women Are Bum Newspapermen," were made to look authentic by scriptwriters Roy Chanslor, Lillie Hayward, and Laird Doyle, all of whom had solid newspaper backgrounds. Adela Rogers St. Johns, one of Hearst's greatest newshens, was enlisted by Warners' PR department to disseminate stories and interviews ensuring everyone that Bette Davis's Ellen Garfield was put through her paces in the best tradition of tabloid sob sisters. She even had a phone interview with the legendary William Randolph Hearst, who confirmed that Davis as Garfield was the real deal.

The fact that Hearst had moved Marion and his Cosmopolitan Productions to Warners after a squabble with Metro-Goldwyn-Mayer over their refusal to place his mistress, Marion Davies, in "stature" roles was largely overlooked by the general public. "I'd hire her at any time," Hearst said. "She can begin with the San Francisco Examiner!"" Jack Warner was overjoyed with the attention, and Davis began receiving invites to Hearst's mansion in San Simeon.

Davis's second film, Special Agent, with George Brent, was a flop. Its sloppy direction by William Keighley irritated her. Sid Hickox, one of her least favourite photographers, shot her without the care and attention Polito and others had showered on her.

In The New York Times, Frank S. Nugent stated succinctly but pointedly:

"In Special Agent, the Warner brothers have produced another of their machine-gun sagas of crime and punishment that is crisp, fast-paced, and thoroughly entertaining." ...It's all been done before, but it never ceases to be visually exciting. ...George Brent personifies the Internal Revenue Service admirably in his reflection of modern manners. Ricardo Cortez is completely believable as the racket lord, and Bette Davis fits in quite well as the patriotic bookkeeper who double-crosses her boss for Uncle Sam and Mr. Brent (in a roughly 05-95 ratio)."

When viewed today, the film does not hold up well, and Davis's role appears to be unnecessary to the plot. The 76-minute runtime is haphazardly edited; Production Code regulations, which were prevalent in 1935, prompted the reshooting of some scenes, which were awkwardly inserted, resulting in jagged continuity. Working from an idea by Martin Mooney, screenwriters Laird Doyle and Abem Finkel do not bring the characters into clear psychological perspective, and motivations are not convincingly assigned.

Brent, who lacked vanity and star desire, normally went through his portions and received his salary without complaint. He was known around the studio as "Apple of Jack Warner's Eye" and "Good Old Mr. Dependable." He said he didn't like most of his films, but he was particularly harsh on Special Agent, telling Ruth Waterbury of Photoplay that it was "a poor, paltry thing, unbelievable and unconvincing in all its aspects." Ruth later told me that Warner's publicity talked her out of using the quotes for fear of affecting the film's chances. "It was one of those rare instances where George spoke his mind for print," she explained, "because he had experienced early adversity in Ireland, and a decent paycheck went a long way with George." He never thought much of his acting abilities and once told me that he was terrified people would discover how bad he was and fire him, so he avoided making waves."

Waterbury also remembered Davis having a crush on Brent

throughout 1935 and making no secret of it.

"The onscreen chemistry between them was always exciting," Waterbury recalled. "And the chemistry offscreen is even better!" But for many years, it was on Bette's side rather than George's. She finally received her reward-reciprocity-after years of waiting! Even then, I had the impression she was more emotional than he was. Of course, George maintained-at least on the surface-his perplexed, aloof approach toward women, which they took to like catnip. Women, whether they confess it or not, don't like to be overly confident in a man, and Bette was no exception."

During this time, Davis had to deal with the uninvited visits of a dangerously neurotic young Warner actor who could compete with Owsley and Clive—and then some!

Davis's Warners teammate, Ross Alexander, was a troubled, befuddled young man. He had gone on the stage at sixteen (a year older than Davis) in 1923, and had been seduced by several older performers and two major stage directors, and had been kept "between engagements" by a series of affluent men. Ross, who was opportunistic and self-deprecating, despised his homosexuality and later went on a crazy overcompensation swing by romancing various famous ladies. He was drawn to strong women, and after joining Warners in 1933, he developed a crazy crush (which Jerry Asher described as an obsession) on Davis. "He was always trying to get cast in a movie with her," Jerry recalled. "It was really pathetic, and so deceptive, when he went on about how if he ever held her in his arms and kissed her onscreen, he'd elicit a wild response from her." I knew enough about Bette to know that Ross wasn't her type. He was a nice-looking lad with a good body and a witty, offhand, sarcastic charm that worked well in certain parts, but she could always recognize a bisexual component in a man, which she needed like a hole in the head at that point. And he wouldn't have been manly enough for her—not that he was effeminate; he wasn't, but there was something feminine and feline about the way he presented himself on screen, particularly in comedic roles."

Ross Alexander appears to have begun penning Davis love letters, which he snuck under her dressing-room door. "She'd read them, laugh at them, and throw them in the wastebasket," Jerry Asher explained. "Ross was a real masochist." He didn't know when he was getting a no—a very loud no—for an answer, and Bette's marriage to Ham Nelson didn't appear to upset him at all."

Ham tried to avoid Davis's sets and the studio itself, but one afternoon he went looking for her and found a note addressed to "MY BELOVED ONE, BETTE," on the envelope. The quick-tempered, jealous Ham tore open the envelope and read the letter. Ross had worded it in such a way that it appeared he and Bette had made love. Of course, they never did, but a furious Ham confronted Davis with it on the set of Satan Met a Lady, a film she was working on with Warren William. He grabbed her behind a flat and demanded to know why. Davis snickered as he read the letter. "That queer is having pipe dreams," she said to her spouse. "He's trying to prove his manhood—or something—and he knows I see right through him." Ham clenched his fists, and Davis replied, "I've got to get back to the set—deal with him as you see fit." Simply get him off my back!"

When Ham went looking for Ross, he discovered him alone in a men's room. "It's my wife you're writing that slush-and-mush to, and she wants no part of it!" he shoved him against the wall. You'll back off if you're any kind of man!" Ross attempted to protect himself by lifting his fists, but Ham, who was larger and stronger, knocked him to the ground.

Ross was unable to begin filming his next feature due to the accompanying black eye. He stayed at home, ruminated, and drank. When she discovered his half-finished notes to Davis under his desk blotter, Ross's wife, Anne Nagel, a pretty young actress who had fallen completely in love with him, left him numerous times.

Ross' infatuation worsened. Davis, becoming increasingly irritated, began mocking him when their paths met, casting aspersions on his manhood. "She's a ruthless b*tch!"" Ross yelled at Jerry Asher. "No, Ross," Jerry said, "she just wants you off it!" Look, you've known some great women, including Anne. You can't possibly acquire them all! Bette is a married woman, and you're simply inviting Ham's wrath!"

Ross began to have bouts of intense depression. He drove out, picked up a male hobo on the side of the road, and had sex with him. The individual threatened Ross with blackmail, and Ross appealed to the Warners' lawyers, who were able to keep the matter quiet. In January 1937, he committed suicide. Before police and reporters spotted the unsent love letters to Davis, Jack Warner hired somebody to get them out of his residence.

Davis attempted to turn a sow's ear into a silk purse in her final 1935 film, and succeeded-sort of. "I worked like ten men on Dangerous," Davis admitted later.

Dangerous received one of the most intriguing critiques Davis had ever received. E. Arnot Robertson of Picture Post commented, "I think Bette Davis would probably have been burned as a witch if she had lived two or three hundred years ago." She provides the strange impression of being imbued with strength that has no conventional outlet."

After two forgettable, mediocre flops, Dangerous—as soapy, melodramatic, and foolish as its core plot was—offered Davis enough material to charge with her individual and unique skill. Joyce Heath, a self-destructive actress down on her luck, has turned to alcohol and believes she's cursed. No one wants to hire or work with her since she has developed such a terrible image for herself. The persona was based on the late Jeanne Eagels, who wasted her remarkable skill in drink and drugs, as well as a careless lifestyle, before dying in 1929.

Dan Bellows, a wealthy young architect played by Franchot Tone on loan from Metro-Goldwyn-Mayer, takes an interest in the floundering Joyce, dries her out at his country house under the watchful eye of a disapproving housekeeper, Alison Skipworth, and gradually restores her sense of self and ambition. He even pays for her comeback play, and they fall in love. Davis, on the other hand, has a hidden spouse, a weakling (John Eldredge) who still loves her and refuses to divorce her. Davis then drives them both into a tree, saying famously, "It's going to be your life or mine!" I'll be free if you're slain. ..It will no longer matter if I am slain. And if both of us die, good riddance!" He is hurt. She only gets a scratch.

Later, realising she is poison for Tone, she sends him back to his fiancée by assuming a heartlessness that earns his disgust, then goes to the hospital to care for her injured husband after witnessing Tone's wedding to socialite Margaret Lindsay, who has been patiently waiting for him to overcome his "dangerous" addiction-Davis—from across the street. Her comeback, of course, is a smashing success.

Many critics and spectators chuckled at the outrageously contrived climax, let alone the other soapy situations and saccharine dialogue, but everyone took Davis' vivid portrayal of a driven, complex, self-destructive woman seriously.

During production, Davis fell in love with the attractive, aristocratic Franchot Tone, who had moved from the stage to the movies in 1932. He had surrendered his great talents to so-so leading-man roles at Metro-Goldwyn-Mayer for three years and had featured in films with Joan Crawford, whom he later married.

This individual was the catalyst for the legendary Bette Davis-Joan

Crawford dispute. Tone had already earned an homme fatal reputation in New York by 1935, thanks to a rumour that he was the father of a young married stage actress's son—a son who grew up to temporarily become a successful cinema player before going into another field. The physical similarities and acting styles were so striking that this unacknowledged son left the show industry relatively young. When the actress's husband discovered the truth, he allegedly beat up both his wife and Tone. This was neither Tone's first or final encounter with melodrama. Joan Crawford's directors were surprised several times when she arrived on work with various injuries from fights with Tone. She divorced him in 1938 after seeing him deshabillé with a young starlet in his MGM dressing room. Tone had to undergo plastic surgery on his face after a confrontation with toughie actor Tom Neal over his third wife, Barbara Payton, in 1951, when he was forty-seven.

Tone fell in love with Davis in 1935, when she was thirty-one and he was twenty-seven. He wasn't the most attractive actor in town—his head was oddly shaped and his features were far from sculptured—but he exuded a polished masculine aura and had a voice that drive women insane; it "sucked off the consonants and jerked off the vowels," which meant it was rich, deep, and tonally varied.

Joan Crawford, who married Tone before the release of Dangerous, was aware that things were heating up between Tone and Davis on the Warner lot, but she was too busy wrapping up a picture at MGM to monitor what was going on. Davis made the most of the situation.

"There was no doubt about it: she was hot for Tone!""Film producer Harry Joe Brown later stated. "On the set and later in her dressing room, they were all over each other." Davis was so negligent (or perhaps she was being a showoff) that she would leave the door ajar, and when I stopped by to chat about the new set we were shooting, I found them in a very tight (read: compromising) position. And when they saw me, they didn't seem to care! Franchot only chuckled and urged me to close the door as I went out. I got out of there quickly. Tone was ready to marry Joan Crawford, and Bette was still married to that jerk Ham Nelson, and things were getting a little thick."

Davis appeared to have little regard for the contract's moral-turpitude terms. She undoubtedly should have, because the Legion of Decency and the Hays Office were riding high on the better-publicised personalities at the time, and "romantic" incidents carried on too openly could be the end of a career.

Speculation about what Harry Joe Brown actually discovered in Davis's dressing room that day is humorous, because it was well known that one of Franchot Tone's favourite sexual positions was "getting serviced"-or, to put it bluntly, fellated. In fact, that's what Joan Crawford allegedly discovered him doing three years later when she caught him with the starlet—and swiftly filed for divorce.

MGM executive Eddie Mannix, who knew Tone well, told me that Tone had joked that he preferred to be fellated since it was one way to avoid getting a lady pregnant. "I had enough abortions and illegitimate pregnancies in New York to last me a lifetime," she said. "A lot of truth is, as always, spoken in jest," Mannix said, laughing.

Tone, knowing he was a good actor, one of the best in the MGM stable, "resented being shunted to secondary status and discovered that the only way to be Top Man was in proving his sexual and romantic prowess with one dame after another," according to director Alfred E. Green. Over a few drinks, he confided to Green that at Cornell, where he had manoeuvred himself into the presidency of the Dramatic Club, he had been known as the "

The failure of MGM to recognize his talent with genuine major roles was so humiliating to him that, according to Joan Crawford, he worked off his embarrassment and despair by beating her up at home. "I put up with the beatings, but the dressing-room infidelity was too much," Joan told Anita Loos later.

Tone, fortunately for Davis, only demonstrated his love and sexual abilities. It was a standard movie setup: for him, when it was finished, it was over; for her, it was a sharp regret. After a day of on- and off-screen romance with vibrant Tone, she returned home to a spineless Ham who was profoundly frustrated.

"I am positive that the mutual hatred between Davis and Crawford began then and there, with the Tone thing," publicist Jerry Asher, a close friend of all three, told me in 1965. "Joan resented his meddling with Bette, even after they married, and Bette resented Joan's establishment of top priority in the Tone scheme of things." Of course, nobody considered the fourth party, poor Ham. What he thought was obviously of no consequence!" However, the Davis-Tone combo in Dangerous was the most dynamic for Christmas audiences in 1935, and many fan letters suggested that they be redeemed. "But Joan was having none of that-she kept him strictly under wraps at MGM and in their Brentwood home," Jerry explained, "and Bette seethed, and not in silence!"" Tone was unusually well endowed where it counted, even in a flaccid state, according to Asher, who frequently swam and exercised with him. "His women must have found him to be a real jaw breaker," Jerry said.

9.

The First Oscar-and Its Aftermathf

Davis rose from a sickbed to attend the 1936 Academy Awards banquet, where she was presented with her Oscar for Dangerous by the legendary D. W. Griffith, who received a special prize on that occasion for his many silent-era classics.

Given the lavishness of the occasion, her casual dress drew considerable criticism. The male winner, Victor McLaglen (for The Informer), donned a white tie and tails, while all the women wore evening dresses, except Davis, who wore a plain print dress with inappropriately large lapels. It was ill-fitting, the kind of thing you'd wear for a casual afternoon of shopping, and it enraged Ruth Waterbury, now the editor of Photoplay.

During the evening, Ruth pulled Bette into the ladies' room and scolded her for arriving to the dinner dressed as she did. Ruth told me she believed Davis was belittling the Academy by awarding her a consolation prize for a film she didn't like instead of one for the well-deserved winner, Of Human Bondage. "I think she did it deliberately," Ruth recounted. "It was her way, possibly unconsciously, of telling the Academy that it wasn't all that important in her scheme of things," Davis later explained. She recalls having nothing proper to wear, so she chose the print, despite her mother's impeccable attire. One wonders why Ruthie didn't take charge before the occasion and demand that Davis look like a winner, especially given they had dressed together the night before.

Davis accepted her late award with humility, claiming that the genuine winner for 1935 should have been Katharine Hepburn for Alice Adams. Her admiration for Hepburn's appearance, acting technique, and way of life was boundless, albeit decades later, when Hepburn had won four Oscars to her two, Davis would temper her praise substantially.

Davis began 1936 with another main role opposite Leslie Howard.

In retrospect, it's not clear why Davis was so excited about landing the role of Gabrielle Maple in The Petrified Forest, the film adaptation of the successful Broadway play starring Leslie Howard.

Humphrey Bogart, who played coldblooded mobster Duke Mantee in the play, rose to popularity, and he reprised his character in the film to great acclaim.

The prestige features of the play most likely appealed to Davis, who reasoned that a less-than-stellar performance in a "prestige" production was still preferable to a lead in a turkey or an also-ran soaper. The role of Gabrielle, on the other hand, might have been performed by a variety of contract actors, including Margaret Lindsay, who works as a server at an Arizona gas station-restaurant and dreams of a painting career and a trip to Paris. It's a dreamy part with no really intense combative events. Davis would have turned down the opportunity if she hadn't been so desperate for a "big" role. If she didn't realise it, Jack Warner was half-embarrassed, half-scornful when she thanked him lavishly for Forest. "I think I like Bette more when she's squabbling and fussing." "Gratitude and sweetness aren't her thing," he told Hal Wallis.

Howard, of course, was at home as the dreamy wanderer whose idealism and impracticality have consigned him to the role of outsider. Bogart, who played the gangster who kidnaps Davis, Howard, his father Porter Hall, grandfather Charley Grapewin, and a couple of passengers and holds them hostage, benefited the most from the picture, landing him a Warner Brothers contract.

Charles Kenyon and Delmer Daves adapted Robert E. Sherwood's fairly turgid and pretentious play for the film. The location shooting and realistic gas-station set on a huge Warner stage created the right atmosphere, but there was no denying that the strong Mantee confrontations were a major selling point in both play and film.

Throughout the production of this, their second picture together, Davis sent confusing signals regarding her personal connection with Howard. He had certainly developed respect for her since Bondage, as she had given a lot of outstanding performances, but he alternated between ignoring her and making vulgar approaches, according to Dick Foran and director Archie Mayo. Davis alleged that he chewed on her arm while hugging her in one intimate session. She may have misinterpreted this as an acting technique on his behalf, given Howard had previously stated that she was not his type. Because he was a notorious womaniser (Olivia De Havilland had a hard time fending him off in the third Davis-Howard film, It's Love I'm After, a year later), one is tempted to trust Howard's version of events.

Aside from the poetic observations about outsiders and insiders, The Petrified Forest seemed to reflect Sherwood's philosophical and dramatic perplexity more than anything else, and Davis's obvious efforts to bring Gaby Maple to life can be seen in the finished picture. This was simply not the type of forceful part in which she could shine; yes, she had played sensitive, warm ladies in earlier and later films, but these roles had more depth and solidity written into them. Gaby is, after all, a romantic young girl searching for space to express her poetic visions, and as portrayed, she is a pallid supporting role for the two strong male characters.

Davis, as usual, expressed her hatred for Bogart, whom she deemed rough, bossy, and moody, but this could have been due to her disappointment that he had the better role. Dick Foran, a former football player, told me in 1964 that he felt quite self-conscious playing her spurned suitor. "I never felt like a big-league actor," he admitted, "and I felt I was out of my league with Davis, Howard, and Bogart." I could tell Bette wasn't feeling well; she was sick a lot, had some injuries on the gas station scene that threw her off form for days, and I didn't think she was thrilled with the photo. One reason was that she had a strong desire to be in the spotlight all the time, and I thought she was pushed to the sidelines for the main event. True, she gets to hold Howard after he is shot by Bogart in his death scene, but he hogs the scene."

The New York Times attempted to see the bright side of Davis's characterization shift in "Forest, but Frank Nugent's assessment that "Bette Davis. ..illustrates that she does not need to be hysterical to make an excellent performance."

In 1966, Archie Mayo recalled Davis being difficult to direct because she was frustrated by Gaby's basic passivity. "Passivity and sweetness were not that girl's strong cards," he said, "and I think she realised she was getting short-changed after she got into the picture." She tried to blame me, but it was the screenwriters who should have been pursued!"

Davis found it embarrassing that her next film was titled, of all things, Cream Princess. She believed the title was obscene and highly suggestive, and she bemoaned the fact that the Legion of Decency and the Production Code rushed in to edit everything else yet didn't even raise an eyebrow at that title!

After all, it was based on Michael Arlen's play about a cosmetics heiress (cream, you see) who is actually a waitress masquerading as the heiress because the firm's publicity man believes her well-publicised amorous exploits will help sales. She is interviewed by a no-nonsense newsman, George Brent, and persuades him to marry her so that he may finish his work, which has been postponed for financial reasons, and she can be free of money hunters like penniless Count Gulliano (Ivan Lebedeff). Of course, her impersonation is found in due order, but the captivated Brent couldn't care less and whisks her away to his mountain house to finish that manuscript and break her into hausfrau habits.

Alfred E. Green, who was frequently heckled and put-upon by the irritated and exasperated Davis, made a valiant effort to steer things in a lively direction, W. A magnificent musical score by Franke Harling and Heinz Roemheld was greater than the film merited, and Charles Kenyon's screenplay pushed hard for humour and sass—but to no avail.

Cream Princess, which was subsequently retitled by an embarrassed Warners to the more sanitary—but also inexplicable—The Golden Arrow, was a massive flop. Davis' admirers from all around the country came in to question why she wasn't given better material. Davis, in one of her typical outbursts of rage, stormed into Jack Warner's office with a basket of such letters and dumped them on the floor in front of him. "Later rumours had it that I had dumped them right on his desk," she said Ruth Waterbury in 1955, "but that wasn't true." I thought the floor worked just as well. I suppose he even read some of them, which didn't help me."

What made The Golden Arrow and its banal hijinks even more painful was the fact that she had won the Academy Award for Dangerous just six weeks before its release—and here she was, following that major achievement with one of the most mundane, foolish, trivial pictures of her career.

"The Golden Arrow was definitely one of the deciding factors in my Big Revolt Against Warners later in 1936," she declared a few days later. "I figured that if after all this time, Arrow was the best I could get, some drastic measures were being called for."

The Davis-Brent moments were acted with terrific bravura and dispatch, as well as a loving simpatico that radiated from the screen. "If only the dialogue and situations had been supportive, but they weren't!"", lamented the San Francisco Examiner reviewer.

"In her first motion picture since winning the Academy Award for best performance of 1935, Bette Davis departs abruptly from the dramatic role and undertakes a straight comedy characterization heavily underscored with romance with the same brisk manner and swift utterance that has marked her career," Motion Picture Herald wrote, "with the same brisk manner and swift utterance that has marked her career." ...The plot is action-packed and fast-paced, seldom veering into the serious."

Throughout the film, Davis was also dissatisfied with George Brent's continued lack of responsiveness or, perhaps, prudence. In 1936, his customary remark was, "You're a married woman, Bette."

In her autobiography, Davis recalls the tragic fate of Satan Met a Lady in the following way: "When the company scheduled [the film], a Dashiell Hammett remake that was not to achieve any quality until John Huston directed it years later under the title The Maltese Falcon, I was so distressed by the whole tone of the script and the vapidity of my part that I marched up to [Jack Warner's] office and demanded that I be given work that was commensurate with my proven ability." Put off—for the time being.

Before settling on the title, Satan Met a Lady was known as The Man in the Black Hat, Hard Luck Dame, and Men on Her Mind. It was first released in 1931 under its original title, The Maltese Falcon, starring Ricardo Cortez as Sam Spade and Bebe Daniels as the Mystery Woman. (Decades later, to avoid confusion with the 1941 version, it was presented on television under the title Dangerous Female.) The Davis-William version, with its infinite title changes, was made in 1936. Then, in 1941, John Huston's masterpiece cemented Humphrey Bogart's superstardom and earned more accolades for Mary Astor, who won a supporting Oscar that year for her performance in Davis' The Great Lie.

Alison Skipworth appeared with Davis and William, playing the role that "Fat Man" Sidney Greenstreet subsequently immortalised—an fascinating characterization sex change. Instead of the famous falcon featured in the previous two versions, the pièce de résistance was a ram's horn adorned with precious diamonds. As Sam Spade's loving and protective secretary, Marie Wilson was allowed free freedom in one of her classic comic roles. Warren William's Sam Spade (renamed Ted Shane in Satan Met a Lady) lacks the actual toughness and cynicism that Bogart so masterfully limned. Davis's character was poorly written and underutilised, and her entrances and exits appear irregular and perplexing. One bright spot for Davis: Warren William had clearly lost interest in her and said only ten words to her throughout the shooting, as she subsequently recalled, half-ruefully, half-relievedly. "Of course, I was twenty-eight years old by then," she chuckled, "and everyone knew he liked them really young and really fresh!"''

The plot of the 1936 version is, at best, perplexing: Valerie (the Davis character) ends up murdering Skipworth's contact man in order to obtain the ram's horn. In the hopes of benefiting herself, she subsequently prevents William's Spade from collecting the $10,000 reward by turning herself into the train's lavatory attendant. When Jack Warner watched the finished product (poorly directed by William Dieterle, who couldn't make head nor tail of the many shenanigans), he was so perplexed by the plot that he ordered a re editing by Warren Low, which delayed the film's release by several months.

The young New York Times critic Bosley Crowther (later one of my guides and mentors) certainly spelled it all out clearly and concisely in a pricelessly accurate—and acid—review worth quoting at length, nailing down Satan Met a Lady's various ineptitudes and Davis's unjust treatment by all hands. Crowther stated:

"The film's ingredients are so disconnected and lunatic, its people so irrelevant and monstrous, that one lives through it expecting to see a group of uninformed individuals appear suddenly from behind the furniture and take the entire cast into protective custody." There is no story, only a jumble of rubbish portraying a succession of studio compromises with an untenable script.``

"Without taking sides in a controversy of such titanic proportions, it is no more than gallantry to observe that if Bette Davis had not recently effectively espoused her own cause against the Warners by quitting her job, the Federal Government would have had to step in and do something about her," Bosley continued. After seeing Satan Met a Lady, all rational people must admit that a 'Bette Davis Reclamation Project' (BDRP) to prevent the wasting of this brilliant lady's talents would not be a dramatic addition to our many initiatives for natural resource conservation."

When Bos Crowther wrote those lines, he was thirty-one years old. Years later, at the age of sixty, he remembered the fear he and his critics felt when Satan opened in New York. "God, it brought out the knight in shining armour in all of us male reviewers, as well as the protective mother in the female reviewers." We all gathered together and issued the notices to England and Davis all at once."

The Davis-in-rebellion illness extended to others connected with the doomed project, much to Jack Warner's amazement. Warren William, a competent actor who had previously been a Warner "reliable" (meaning he'd take any piece of crap thrown at him without complaint), stood up to Jack Warner like a man one day and told him "no more!" Warner might break his contract, suspend him, do whatever he wanted, but he, too, would not see his genius "monstrously debased and corrupted," as he put it grandiloquently. Following that, director William Dieterle marched up to the inner sanctum and said that he would join Davis as far away as England itself, if necessary, if the skills he had cultivated in Europe and America were not put to better use. "Christ, that scumbag has started a rebellion!"" Warner sighed.

10.

The Great Rebellion-and the Return

In the mid-1930s, Bette Davis, having completed "Satan Met a

Lady," declined a role in "God's Country and the Woman," unimpressed by its early Technicolor. Her refusal led to an extended strike against Warner Bros. During this time, Jack Warner hinted at a role in "Gone With the Wind," but Davis, disillusioned by Warner's unfulfilled promises, dismissed the opportunity, a decision she later regretted.

Retreating to Laguna Beach, Davis rejected several scripts, resulting in a suspension from Warner Bros. Meanwhile, British producer Ludovico Toeplitz offered Davis a role in "I'll Take the Low Road" and a subsequent film with Maurice Chevalier, both to be shot in Europe. Davis accepted, but Warner Bros. intervened legally, preventing her from working with other studios. A legal battle ensued in England, with Warner Bros. eventually winning, forcing Davis to return to Hollywood and resume her contract.

Back in Hollywood, Davis found a changed atmosphere at Warner Bros., thanks in part to George Arliss's intervention. Warner agreed to cover most of her legal costs and offered her "Marked Woman," a film she found satisfactory. Despite her struggles, Davis continued to work with Warner Bros., taking roles in various films, including "Kid Galahad" and "It's Love I'm After," though she often felt underutilised or mis-cast.

Throughout this period, Davis faced challenges both professionally and personally, including financial strains and artistic frustrations. However, her determination and talent eventually led to a resurgence in her career, as she continued to seek roles that matched her abilities and ambitions.

11.

Bette O'Hara?

The reasons why Bette Davis was denied the role of Scarlett O'Hara in Gone With the Wind remains a mystery to this day. Davis, like everyone else, has a tale to tell.

In the spring of 1936, Jack Warner encouraged her to be a "good girl" and write God's Country and the Woman for him in exchange for a chance at "a great new book" he had optioned. Davis, unimpressed, sneered, "I'm sure it's a pip!"" and stormed out the door for London and her lawsuit. The irony was that Jack, at long last, was offering her a position and a picture that would have been ideal for her if she had only paused long enough to look into it deeper. True, there was a good reason for her behaviour at the time. But, because Jack had sent her so many false alarms about future parts, Davis reasoned that he was duping her once more with another enticing chimaera—all in order to recruit her immediate participation with the project at hand.

Gone With the Wind had been published to great acclaim while she was in London, and Jack Warner, in an act of terrible judgement, had sold the option rights to David O. Selznick. Several factors may have influenced him, including Davis' disdain for it (despite the fact that she had not read it and knew nothing about it) and his personal belief that GWTW production expenses would exceed the Warner budget due to its length and complexity.

By 1937, Selznick was conducting a worldwide search for the appropriate actor to play Rhett Butler, the soldier of fortune with the sexual allure and self-assurance that women fear but crave like catnip, and Scarlett O'Hara, the headstrong southern beauty that all men covet. Scarlett, who is perverse, ambitious, and a natural survivor, resists Rhett's love for her to the very end, only to lose it-for a time; tomorrow, in her famous words, being another day.

Davis had read the novel several times by mid-1937 and was well aware of all the fuss Selznick had made over the quest for the "absolutely right" Scarlett and Rhett. She was ready for another chance and was determined to seize it. Jack Warner understood how desperately she wanted Scarlett, and to punish her for putting him through so much in London the year before, he told her that no loan outs were one of the criteria she had agreed to. David O. Selznick considered Davis a possibility, but he questioned if he could obtain her, and what Jack Warner's terms would be if he did.

Jack proposed a deal: he would lend Davis for Scarlett in exchange for David accepting Errol Flynn as Rhett. If he had to lend, Jack reasoned, why not get two major stars back instead of just one—his savvy showman instinct told him GWTW would be a star-boosting blockbuster for all involved. Davis dominated all fan surveys, and thousands wrote in proclaiming the Fiery Filly from the Burbank lot the Perfect Fiery Filly of GWTW during 1937. But David had doubts, as did George Cukor, the guy who looked to be the director at the moment. Yes, she had the temperament, the iron-strong character, the survivalist toughness, and the passionate tenacity required to pursue Ashley Wilkes, the sweet southern aristocrat who would spend the entire film rejecting her. No one was more temperamentally and creatively qualified than Davis to be the arch-unrequited lover, survivor, mover and shaker in restoring the broken postwar South's commerce. They all agreed that she had it all—except for one thing. Did she possess the breathtaking beauty and dynamic sex appeal to keep dominating, strong-willed, tough realist Rhett Butler pursuing her for ten years? There was reason to be sceptical in that regard.

Davis at Warners learned of this one reservation. She was the first to concede that she was striking rather than attractive, but she insisted in multiple emotional phone calls to Selznick that she could compensate for it with passion, fire, and sheer personality force.

And, as she later demonstrated in other photographs from her heyday, careful camera work and sophisticated makeup could give her the appearance of beauty. Selznick was won over, but George Cukor's decision was delayed.

Davis insisted for years that Cukor was prejudiced against her; he still remembered her as the drab little wren he had met in Rochester a decade ago. This argument is weak, however, because Cukor, a brilliant guy who missed nothing, had observed her remarkable achievements in recent years. Davis was mistaken about Cukor, who agreed with Selznick that she could make personality appear to be "nine tenths of it" and that this Scarlett could be no kitten but a tigress-in-training who had to telegraph her personality straight away, in reel one.

Meanwhile, Selznick kept dropping leads, hints, and even press releases attesting to the fact that he was contemplating many other women in order to keep the media mills churning and the tension at fever pitch. Miriam Hopkins was a true southerner, even in the state where GWTW was set. She would have the Bainbridge, Georgia accent down pat. But Miriam would be approximately thirty-six when they eventually got down to shooting—a little old for a character who was supposed to age from sixteen to twenty-eight. Yes, she's fiery; yes, she's spiteful; sure, she's a powerful character, but she's just too old. Hopkins battled hard for the part. Would GWTW have been in colour if she hadn't done the first colour epic, Becky Sharp, in 1935? Was she not a proven quantity because she had not established that she could dominate a cinematic reproduction of a great novel? The verdict was once again: too old. When Jack and George told her, they were a little more diplomatic; "mature" was the description they used. However, this did not stop the Bainbridge Bitch from trashing furniture and ripping down drapes in the hotel suite where she had been waiting for the ruling.

Then there was Margaret Sullavan, another southerner from Virginia.

In 1935, she and Randolph Scott co-starred for Paramount in So Red the Rose, based on the Stark Young novel, which had a plot and atmosphere comparable to GWTW. Scott was also considered for the role of the courtly, enigmatic Ashley Wilkes, which went to Leslie Howard. Maggie wanted the part, but she married Leland Hayward and had two children in a year and a half, leaving her looking somewhat haggard and overweight at the time.

Cukor's favourite, Katharine Hepburn, was in the running for a while, but she wasn't as beautiful as Scarlett, and her angular, New England aura didn't fit with GWTW's atmosphere, as Cukor eventually admitted. Tallulah Bankhead was also considered, but, like Hopkins, she appeared too old and weathered at thirty-five. She may have gotten the accent perfect because she was from Alabama, but it wasn't enough to save her. Then things got ludicrous, with Joan Crawford expressing interest (Selznick and Cukor moaned and politely declined). Susan Hayward, who was only eighteen at the time, was evaluated but was deemed to be too immature. And so it went, with Selznick's dramatic "search" garnering maximum publicity, much to his delight.

Norma Shearer was the next contender. With Marie Antoinette, the great MGM star proved she could control a lengthy period picture complete with expensive costumes and locations. Selznick really explored making a deal with MGM to borrow her and Clark Gable as a Scarlett-Rhett combo. Shearer was stunning, powerful, and emotionally compelling-but she had two flaws. She, too, would have appeared mature at thirty-seven for Scarlett, having been born in 1900. When her fans found out about her flirting with the character, they wrote so many messages to MGM and Selznick saying that their idol was "too ladylike," "too nice a person" to play spiteful, sensual, vixenish Scarlett, that Miss Shearer graciously resigned.

Meanwhile, Clark Gable was far ahead of his competitors, including Fredric March (at forty, too old and not sexy or insolent enough for

Rhett), Ronald Colman (at forty-five, too civilised and British), and Warner Baxter (again, too old and insufficiently forceful). Gary Cooper was considered, but the chemistry and personality traits did not appear to be quite right.

Which led David and George back to Errol Flynn-this time as one half of a package deal with Davis, courtesy of Jack Warner.

Jack knew in his heart that Errol, as gorgeous, rakish, charming, and sensual as he may be, lacked the "X" element for Rhett. But he was thinking about how GWTW would send Errol back to Warners as an even bigger money-maker. Davis was the one who didn't want Flynn to play Rhett. She told Jack Warner that Errol might be dashing and attractive enough in schlock adventures like Captain Blood and Charge of the Light Brigade, but a dominant, domineering figure like Rhett demanded a man, not a boy, and Flynn was exactly that to her: a charming, flirty, seductive, cute boy. What she didn't tell Jack was that she'd had a crush on Errol when he first appeared in late 1934. Davis saw Flynn as charismatic, seductive, and winning, but also devious, untrustworthy, and a taunting tormentor of women. He wouldn't twist her around his little finger, she'd seen what he did to other women.

As a result, Davis categorically refused to play Scarlett if Flynn played Rhett. It's difficult to think that, after all these years, she would have turned down a part practically written for her solely because of Flynn. She later stated multiple times over the years that his incompetent, lightweight performance would have lowered the quality of her own-but would it have? In the future, it would be revealed that in the two films in which Jack Warner (with his consummate, if crudely executed, irony) was to cast her opposite Flynn, she lifted him up rather than the other way around—so why didn't it occur to her in 1937 that she might have done the same for Flynn with GWTW?

Perhaps she wasn't confident she could carry two people through one film in 1937. Jezebel, while impending, remained in the future. She had not yet risen to prominence among critics and the general public, nor had she achieved complete self-awareness of her abilities. Or perhaps she was already in love with Flynn (who, like herself, was married) and didn't want the emotional excess or strain or whatever the risk included.

Then there was Gable, who was nearly set for Rhett thanks to an MGM loanout. Davis' feelings for him were also ambiguous. She knew he was perfect for Rhett, but she still nursed a grudge against him for saying in 1935 that his co-star Claudette Colbert would have been a far better loanout candidate for It Happened One Night than Davis would have been. "Claudette has the comedy timing, and the expertise," he informed Frank Capra. "Davis is too heavy, too intense; she belongs in drama, not comedy." And she isn't beautiful enough to make an audience think I'd chase her throughout the nation on a bus, as I do in the film." Davis had also heard that Gable had qualms about her portraying Scarlett. "Would Rhett Butler go all out for someone like her?"" To Cukor and Selznick, he laughed. "Rhett Butler—a man capable of commanding the most beautiful women in the world to do his bidding?""

George Cukor, who enjoyed brawls, made certain that Gable's opinion reached Davis, with predictable results. The King had pounced on her supposed lack of beauty. Hadn't she been putting the less skilled "beauties" in their place in Hollywood for six years? She yelled. Who was that big-eared ape thinking he was?

Davis' retaliation did not end with the famed ears. Gable had refused to pin them back, but they still made him uncomfortable. She also mocked his teeth. He got them fixed early in his MGM career, but under the caps they had rotted out of his mouth, so he had the remains taken and had worn dentures, top and bottom, since 1931. When one or the other dropped, his speech took on a peculiar slurryslurpy tone that some of his female fans found seductive. If Franchot Tone swallowed his consonants and jerked his vowels, Gable was doing the same in his own way.

The teeth, the ears. Davis continued to amass evidence against MGM's leading romantic heartthrob, the idol of millions of women. Carole Lombard, later Gable's wife, provided Davis with additional material. Gable appeared to have a slight case of phimosis that he refused to correct-his cock, like his ears, he kept sacred. The phimosis made pulling back the foreskin of his uncircumcised cock so painful that he left it alone most of the time. Smegma odour inevitably collected excessively. Lombard, known for her scatological vulgarisms and flippant obscenities, had even told a press conference that Gable was not only uncircumcised but that his bedmanship was lacking-premature ejaculation being suggested. "Pappy's pee-pee isn't all that big, whether up or down!" Carole told Ruth Waterbury."

Davis had no sexual feelings for Gable, which made it all the easier for her to deploy her accumulated armoury of retaliatory weapons against a guy who, she believed, had snubbed, degraded, and discarded her qualifications for the post she desired above all others.

She then gave Ruth Waterbury of Photoplay, Katherine Albert, and others different versions of the same on-set interview, with Gable as the topic. Her statements were not set down in cold black print since they were unprintable for family or even broad newspapers. They were, nonetheless, widely shared among the Cinemaland Cognoscenti. She spit out, "I can't stand a man who has fake store teeth and doesn't keep his uncircumcised cock clean under the foreskin," adding, "I hear he shoots too soon and messes himself all the time," after stating that she had no regrets about missing out on Gable as a co-star. Are you a great lover? Excellent forgery!"Word of this came back to Gable, as Adela Rogers St. Johns and Ruth Waterbury both informed me, and as Adela put it, "Clark didn't find

Bette any laughing matter after that!"" But, as it turned out, Gable got off lightly. George Cukor could have told Davis that his firing from Gone With the Wind was caused not only by Gable's belief that he was favouring female stars, but also because Cukor knew that Gable had given his famous uncircumcised cock to gay wolf William Haines back in the 1920s, when Haines was a star and Gable was a bit player, in an attempt to gain Haines' support in his upward climb. As a result, working with Cukor made him nervous, especially when Cukor called him "dear" and "honey" on set.

According to Jerry Asher, one funny story, very likely accurate if one knew George, has the scorned director giving Gable a cake of Lifebuoy soap and a small bottle of Listerine for his birthday in 1939. According to Jerry, the accompanying note stated, "Clark fear—the soap is to clean out the cheese beneath your foreskin and the Listerine is to take away the smell." Neither George nor anyone else appears to have gone on record as to how the voraciously oral Billy Haines coped without Listerine or Lifebuoy. Some Hollywood secrets are treasured to the end.

Davis proceeded to rant and rave in interviews, talk shows, and private and not-so-secret chats throughout the years about having "missed out on Scarlett-the role of my life!""

"I only argue with their eventual choice [for Scarlett] because it was not me," she writes in her memoirs. I'm not taking anything away from Miss [Vivien] Leigh's lovely performance when I say I still wish I could have gotten my hands on it!"

But, in the end, Bette Davis was to have the last word—and the ultimate laugh. Her second film, Jezebel, based on the Owen Davis play, not only provided her a similarly strong southern vixen part, but also earned her the 1938 Academy Award, which was announced in the midst of the filming of Gone With the Wind in early 1939.

"Julie Marsden, the Jezebel in question, was Scarlett's blood sister," Davis exclaimed later. She was every inch the southern belle, willful, naughty, and haughty. She possessed the same steely fragility, ingenuity, and rebelliousness. Julie was my favourite part since Mildred."

12.

1939: The Great Year

NEW YEAR 1939 saw Davis reach an all-time professional high, with four films that were both commercial and creative achievements. For her, the year began disastrously.

Davis began Dark Victory (which was released in early 1939) with his physical health exhausted and his emotional health perfect fodder for a psychiatrist. Ham was divorcing her after blackmailing Hughes, her lover. Anatole Litvak, whose continental appeal, vivacity, and love of partying had restored her spirits, was turned off by Davis's gloomy, drab offscreen life, in which she scraped pennies to cover Ruthie's luxury and Bobby's sanitarium expenses. Her regular bouts of despair, psychosomatic symptoms, and fear of public exposure all conspired to have a catastrophic effect on her neurological system.

Her problems were exacerbated when Miriam Hopkins called to remind her that she was still Litvak's wife, despite Davis's preemption of Jezebel. Miriam was calmed down by Jack Warner, who signed her to a new contract after she threatened to identify Davis as a correspondent in her divorce lawsuit against Litvak. She'd been away from the spotlight for nearly a year and was eager to return. Jack offered her prominent roles, including one with Davis herself. "If I ever get into a picture with that husband stealer,"

Hopkins shouted, "I'll show her what acting is all about!""

Warner and Wallis just chuckled when they learned of Miriam's antics. "If the Hopkins dame wants to work up an ongoing bitch feud," Jack Warner chuckled, "let her!" It'll be fantastic PR if we put them together in a picture" (a prophecy that was to come true). Meanwhile, Hopkins was preparing to divorce the all-too-willing Litvak without naming Davis, as Jack Warner had requested. "Marriage with Miriam—an affair with Bette—I've had enough crazy, temperamental women to last me years—now I need a rest, no?" Litvak later explained." Everyone agreed he did.

Davis was so stressed and sickly during the first few weeks of Dark Victory's schedule that she begged Wallis to let her go, stating she was sick and wasn't doing the character credit. But Wallis had only just witnessed the first rushes. "For God's sake, stay sick, Bette," he pleaded, "you're doing fantastic!""

Separate meetings were arranged with director Edmund Goulding and leading man George Brent by Jack Warner, Hal Wallis, and Hal's associate producer, David Lewis. "It's up to you guys to keep the lady on an even keel," Hal said. "Eddie, you work with her—and George, you play with her—and it will keep her excited, entertained, and alert!"" As it turned out, neither man required much convincing; they had each come up with the identical concept on their own.

This was Edmund Goulding's second collaboration with Davis. In That Certain Woman, she had responded nicely to him. He worked with her carefully, soothingly, planning down her overacting, keeping her motions and expressions regulated and on target, confident that her role as the dying heiress Judith Traherne would bring her to the fullest of her skill and the public glory she deserved. Goulding's attitude was delicate, feminine, and empathic, similar to Wyler's in That Certain Woman. Instead of threatening, scolding, and commanding her, he worked with her, giving her the benefit of his insight, letting her laugh delightfully at his clowning—acting out the ardent love-making he expected from Davis with the starring man. Davis gave him a performance every bit as disciplined as Wyler could have given him through subtle indirection and gentle coaxing.

The two filmmakers' styles were very different. One softly persuaded and directed, while the other drove and disciplined; both were equally effective. Davis, however, required careful attention. She went haywire if she was driven too far or too rapidly and strode off to her dressing room. But, as the weeks passed, she began to immerse herself in Judith Traherne, and from that point until the end of the shoot, work was a thrill and an escape from her enormous personal issues.

Offscreen, George Brent complemented Goulding's professional guidance admirably: during the filming of Dark Victory, Davis earned a reward she had coveted for six years—a reciprocation of Brent's sentiments. As he saw Davis's off-screen calamities pile up, he developed a strong sympathy and care for her, which grew into a love for her that eventually became sexual. The two fell in love. Davis' portrayal of Judith was immensely enhanced by the calming romantic and physical addresses from a guy she had always cared profoundly for, acting out night after night at his place or at her Coldwater Canyon house. Jack Warner and Hal Wallis swore columnists Louella and Hedda to secrecy about the romance, because the moral turpitude clauses that Hays and the Legion of Decency may have insisted on implementing could have killed Davis's career.

Tallulah Bankhead's 1934 Broadway drama Dark Victory played for only fifty-one performances before shutting. However, David O. Selznick was intrigued by it and purchased it for $50,000. He explored teaming Greta Garbo and Fredric March in it, as well as other potential outstanding pairings, but eventually lost interest and sold it to Warners in January 1938, who first saw it as a vehicle for Kay Francis. But Kay was afraid of playing a dying woman, and while it was lying around, Davis saw a script, fell in love with it, and pressed hard for it.

Jack Warner was sceptical-who wants to see a film about a woman who kicks off? This was his reaction. "Why go morbid on your audience when you're just getting started?"" he explained to Bette. "All those women out there want to see you making love, vicariously fulfilling their dreams." You then conk out on them!"

But Davis persisted, telling Warner again and over that she needed something she could put her heart into at that juncture, and ultimately Jack, admitting the role was meaty even if the concept made his flesh crawl, urged her, "Okay, go hang yourself!"" and she was cast in the part.

Casey Robinson, the renowned provider of powerful female-interest scripts, truly delivered with Dark Victory. After more than fifty years, the plot is so widely known that only a brief recapitulation is required.

Long Island heiress Judith Traherne enjoys horses, liquor, and men in about that order. She rides the nags, swills champagne, loves the guys, and flutters around her social circle with a false indifference tinted with a profound love of life and adventure. Then she discovers she has a brain tumour and is dying. She believes she is cured after the operation and falls in love with the doctor, George Brent, who doesn't have the heart to tell her she has less than a year to live. When she learns of her death sentence by mistake, she becomes brittle, caustic, and cynically peregrination, but she bravely faces reality, marries the doctor who has fallen in love with her, and gives up her former life to help him with his studies in Vermont. When death arrives, she faces it without pity. Her suffering and eventual death spiritually redeem her and bring forth her best qualities, and hers is truly a win over the dark in the end.

Dark Victory emerges as a magnificent cinematic merging of acting, direction, scripting, and Ernest Haller's photography, thanks to the script, Goulding's coaching, and Davis's determined application of her strongest artistic instincts. And Max Steiner delivers one of his more moving compositions, emphasising Davis' emotional crises and eventual catharsis as only he can.

Davis's worry as she discovers the depth of her situation is captured well in the film, as she stares into a mirror, pushing back her chair and rubbing her brow. When her maid inquires about her headache, she responds, "Yes, a BIG headache!" Please bring me some champagne!"And her expression conveys the wonderfully mobile synthesis of horror, panic, and emotional devastation that she is experiencing at the time." When she discovers Brent lied to her about her condition following the first surgery, she is enraged, dismissive ("Having fun with the knives lately, doctor?"), and heartbrokenly disillusioned by what she believes is merely his sympathy when she thought he had given her his love.

When Jane and Brent reconnect and marry, she is bright, breezy, and active on the farm in Vermont, where they've agreed not to obsess about the Great Inevitable due in months or weeks. Davis is planting hyacinths in the garden with best friend Geraldine Fitzgerald (wonderfully sympathetic and sensitive in her role of Greek Chorus-style supportive) just before Brent's departure for a medical conference in New York (he is researching her disease) when she recognizes the sudden dimming of her vision that she has been told will precede her demise by only a few hours. The sun is shining brightly, but she thinks it has darkened before recognizing its warmth on her hands. Sudden terror and dismay are quickly overshadowed by a brave determination that Brent will not see her die; she sends him away, climbs the stairs, and prays to a Max Steiner alarm of angel sounds before lying on the bed-to a slow fading of the film's focus.

Davis' technique is consistent and solid throughout. She plays Judith Traherne, putting everything of her career's hardships and disappointments, all of the volatility and horror of her romantic and marital disasters, all of the newfound resignation of a spirit that has transcended adversity through wisdom and peace, into it. Judith Traherne is one of the most vivid creations of the film, as filtered through the strong yet disciplined creative skills of one of the screen's premier artists.

When Dark Victory first premiered in April 1939, critics were delighted. "It's [Davis'] show, her special kind of show, all the way through," wrote James Shelley Hamilton in the National Board of Review Magazine (predecessor of Films in Review). .."She has never before seemed to be so completely inside a part, with every mannerism and physical aspect of her suited to its expression," noted Frank Nugent in The New York Times. Moreover, she is bewitched and charming."

"Admittedly, it is a great role-rangy, full-bodied, designed for a virtuoso, almost certain to invite the faint damning of 'tour de force.' But that must not detract from the eloquence, tenderness, heart-breaking sincerity with which she has played it." We do not denigrate an actress for remarking on her excellent chance; what counts is that she took advantage of it."

Davis was set to receive yet another Academy Award nomination for Dark Victory. She did, however, lose the award for Best Actress in 1939 to the actress who had gotten the role she so sorely desired, Vivien Leigh for Scarlett O'Hara.

Dark Victory was also her one and only appearance alongside Ronald Reagan. He is simply a supporting actor in this; a weak, alcoholic, aimless but affable young playboy who listens to her problems with ironic sympathy and even suggests a prospective romantic interest, which is given short shrift in the script. Ronald

Reagan, then twenty-eight years old, was at the pinnacle of his youthful all-American lad romantic appeal. After a stint as a Midwestern sports broadcaster, he had a terrific voice, looked great in swimming trunks, and was widely sought after by various ladies, the most of whom were actresses.

His role, as written by Casey Robinson, was merely that of Judith Traherne's thoughtless, aimless, mildly likeable young playboy pal, but Edmund Goulding, always on the lookout for the manly charms of attractive studs, took a shine to Reagan, then developed a crush on him, which clean-cut, solidly heterosexual Reagan uneasily sensed. Things became strained when Goulding began coaching Reagan in his character, insisting on effete, effeminate details in his performance. Reagan protested, and Goulding, irritated and feeling indirectly rejected, continued to scold him. Reagan subsequently remembers Goulding making him feel inadequate, shallow, and uneducated. The feyness that Goulding intended Reagan to convey in his character was certainly inappropriate for both Reagan the man and Reagan the actor. His instincts informed him that the part should be regarded as just another spoiled-brat bubblehead on the verge of drunkenness, with far too much money and leisure time for his own benefit. In the end, his will triumphed over Goulding's, for which he was never forgiven.

George Brent was to remain Davis's protector and forbearer for a whole year; he became her shoulder to cry on and lean on, and she was eternally thankful to him for it. Brent, being only human, was frequently irritated by his lover's high-strung, over-emphatic, and superelectric approach to matters great and small—and finally, even he grew tired of the emotional wear and tear. Davis had revealed that she truly wanted to marry Brent, but he didn't think marriage would work for them-a sensible decision in retrospect. Brent was on a sabbatical from marriage after the Chatterton divorce, except for two very brief trips to the altar with Ann Sheridan and Constance Worth.

He doubted marriage fit his temperament. Davis was distraught, and her sentiments of rejection were exacerbated.

Geraldine Fitzgerald has always been complimentary of Bette Davis. "I've remained friends with Bette to this day," she told Rex Reed in 1971. We both had to travel to Hollywood recently for work, so we decided to take the train and catch up. Crowds would gather around her in every place, and she would act like a queen, pretending not to notice all the commotion. She'd keep asking about every male on the old Warners lot, and I'd respond, 'Well, I never had an affair with him,' to which she'd yell, 'Well, you're the only one who didn't, Fitzie!'"

Geraldine told Doug McClelland in 1976, "We used to sit around the [Dark Victory] set and say, 'I don't think it's going to work.' A lot was improvised, and Eddie Goulding rewrote a lot of it." In fact, he created my entire character-she wasn't in the original theatre play-as a sort of Greek chorus for the dying heroine, so she wouldn't have to whine so much."

Geraldine said Goulding asked her, "What would you do in real life under those circumstances?" while she and Davis were gardening and Davis felt blindness coming on and that her death was imminent." She said that she had always been afraid of death and that she would most likely flee. "He told me to do just that; I did, and it's in the movie." (Geraldine's memory of this is slightly skewed, because Davis's character insists on her leaving in order to save her the drama of a heartbreaking goodbye.)

Geraldine assured Doug McClelland that Davis was not tough to deal with—at least not with her. When it was time for her to climb the stairs to die softly and resignedly in her chamber, she remembered asking Eddie Goulding, much to everyone's amusement, "Well, Eddie, am I going to act this or is Max?"" "She admired Max Steiner, whose music complimented her performances so beautifully, and in this case she was joking," she added hastily, continuing, "She always played fair with her other performers, never tried to divert your face away from the camera, as so many did." [Did Geraldine have Miriam Hopkins in mind at that point?] She would not have considered such behaviour to be moral. And she understood it would be better for the movie if everyone pitched."

Geraldine defended some of the positions Davis accepted about 1976, saying, "Some people today say she takes any role-but I can tell you, although maybe I shouldn't, that she supports armies of people."

Geraldine was defending her friend to everyone who would listen as late as 1987. "She's had a brave and heroic life-she's the most resilient, toughly elastic person I know." And nearly eighty at that! Other people are settling down to relax far before that age, but not Better—or me! Maybe I got a cue from her. Anyone would be inspired by her!" In between directing scenes in one of her most recent plays, Geraldine told me, "Dark Victory will always be seared on my memory as one of my most sublime experiences-thanks to her." You were caught up in something bigger than yourself when you acted with her-that was Bette-larger than life in the greatest meaning of that now-cliched term. That's one of the secrets to her long-lasting, far-reaching artistic influence!"

"[The film] is about two things, love and death, and I decided [when writing the film] that these two elements should be kept apart as long as possible; that when there was a scene about love, it wasn't about death, and when there was a scene about death, it wasn't about love," Casey Robinson said in 1979, forty years later. On the surface, this appears to be the case. So when there was a love scene, death was beneath it; when there was a death scene, love was beneath it-all the while, until the very end, when one would recombine them into a sort of requiem."

Davis was seen to best advantage in the second of her blockbuster 1939 films, Juarez, as Carlotta, empress of Mexico and consort of the ill-fated Emperor Maximilian, the Austrian archduke who is duped by Napoleon III into accepting the crown through a rigged plebiscite in order to further Napoleon's machinations for collecting Mexican debts to France.

Davis's Carlotta, always emotionally unstable and superintense, travels to Europe to beg Napoleon to help her husband put down Juarez's resurgent forces, but Napoleon, intimidated by the post-Civil War United States' determination to invoke the Monroe Doctrine with force if necessary, declines. This provides Davis with the opportunity for one of her most iconic angry sequences, in which she denounces Napoleon in front of his wife and ministers before fainting, foreshadowing her gradual decline into lunacy. Davis goes insane with a colourful fury in a horrific moment later in the film, easily outdoing her wild performance in Bordertown. She is delirious and pitiful as she tells Metternich (Walter Kingsford) that the "evil" Napoleon is haunting her and that "they" are going to harm her. Davis paints a vivid, gripping portrait of a woman who was never physically or psychologically strong to begin with but summons manic energy (which eventually destroys her) in her desperation to save the life and wealth of a beloved spouse in these and other moments.

Though Paul Muni and Bette Davis co-starred in this colourful and spectacular historical drama (his name took precedence), they never met. His, her, and her husband's stories are conveyed in a counterpunctual manner, using smart intercutting and parallel action techniques. Some argue that it is two separate scripts, but a careful examination of the film reveals that one cannot exist without the other-for both dramas are poignant explorations of character and motivation that feed upon each other, both to highlight contrasts and illuminate the tragic human motivations and drives that drive one,

Juarez, to eventual victory and the other, Maximilian, to defeat and execution.

Juarez is a thrilling, colourful historical drama directed by William Dieterle, a sensitive artist with a keen eye for grandiose material like this. Erich Wolfgang Korngold's soundtrack is gripping, cleverly blending Mexican and Austrian motifs for heart-stopping results. Juarez is film at its most ornate, with all the greatest technological accoutrements that the various screen artisans had acquired as of 1939. It is one of the great masterpieces of the screen, beautifully acted by the principals, touching in its intimate scenes, deeply moving in its pageantry and intense evocation of conflicting national ideals-monarchist versus republican-and has been unfairly downgraded over the years by people whose political obsessiveness overshadows their esthetic appreciation. Certainly, Juarez eloquently embraces the democratic process, like in the scene where Muni's Juarez explains the difference between a monarchy and a republic to the impulsive but well-meaning young general Diaz (John Garfield). Muni, who is severely made up to resemble the stolid Indian features of the legendary Juarez, is terrific throughout, lending strength, firmness, and iron purpose to his character.

Both Davis and John Huston have attempted to blame Muni for "hogging" the film in their respective autobiographies, with Davis claiming that he added "fifty pages to the script" and Huston, who co-wrote the screenplay with Aeneas MacKenzie and Wolfgang Reinhardt, insisting that Muni's ego drove him to force changes in his favour, even assigning his brother-in-law, screenwriter Abem Finkel, to carry them out. However, the end effect appears to contradict this. Carlotta and Maximilian in their halves, and Juarez in his, appear to share the meal of exquisite drama, spectacle, and human poignancy that this excellent film provides. The final cut is 125 minutes long, yet the great pacing and fascinating drama make it seem to fly by in half an hour.

Brian Aherne, who plays Maximilian, provides his best performance yet. Aherne, a veteran of the London stage and Broadway, had made an initial splash in films as Marlene Dietrich's sculptor-lover in the 1933 Song of Songs, and had followed this up with solid leading-man stints opposite such great ladies of drama as Helen Hayes, Joan Crawford, and Merle Oberon when he was only twenty-nine years old. His Maximilian is a heartfelt performance, sympathetic and gentle, yet aware of his monarchical destiny and resolved to rule justly in the interests of all his people. When it is his turn to explain to Garfield's Diaz the proper tasks of a king in a just society, he, too, is moved.

All three stars get at least one inning, and comparing the merits of Aherne's, Davis', and Muni's delineations is like comparing apples, oranges, and pears. Davis' depiction is likely the most vivid of the three. Her Carlotta is intense, passionate, and frantic, perpetually poised on the razor's edge of instability that leads to tragic lunacy. In her wild-eyed, strongly expressed pleadings to Claude Rains' Napoleon, and even in her grief-stricken, self-denying address to her husband, she offers to walk away to give him an opportunity to meet someone else who will give him an heir; she indirectly hints at her final fate. In a delicate, deeply felt love scene, he declines the offer because he loves her so much. Later, to assure the dynasty's survival, they adopt a Mexican-born boy as their "crown prince." However, Napoleon's deliberate withdrawal from his failed Mexican mission leaves Maximilian and his few dedicated followers and motley "Imperial Army" at the mercy of the ever-advancing local Mexican forces led by the implacable Juarez.

If there is a flaw, it is in the tacked-on ending at a cathedral, where Muni begs forgiveness while looking down at Aherne's executed body in a coffin. Despite Muni's and the audience's realisation that Maximilian is a kind man with the best of intentions, it is completely fake and uninspired.

Davis remembered the film as her first introduction to the actor Claude Rains, whom she admired and admired for the rest of her life. She remembered the imperial study scene in which she chastises him for betraying his covenant with her husband and yells, "Murderer!" Murderer!" Rains' Napoleon gazed at her with such venomous hatred as he scornfully rebuffed her that she was convinced he was expressing genuine contempt for her acting efforts. Of course, this was not the case, since Rains regarded Davis' abilities in high regard, and they enjoyed working together in three more films.

Claude Rains arrived in Hollywood in 1933, following brilliant years on the London stage and Broadway, particularly in characterizations in which he excelled thanks to the Theatre Guild. He wasn't seen for the majority of his debut performance, the 1933 Invisible Man, but the bandaged figure was unmistakably Rains, given the incomparable voice and the distinctive bravura stance. The often-married Rains cut a wide swath in the Hollywood of the 1930s and 1940s, giving even character roles with minimal film the punch of a star presence. Davis and Rains become close friends throughout the years. When asked if Rains was a "happy" man after his death by a TV talk-show host, Davis offered an elegant answer to the effect that no complicated artist was ever happy in the conventional meaning of the word, that people who felt and thought deeply could find relief only through art-or words to that effect. Davis certainly displayed her comprehension of the artist's psyche and esthetic in her understanding of the intricate gifts of the incomparable, irreplaceable Claude Rains.

Rains' Napoleon is the best portrayal of the historical Napoleon's nephew, who began as a revolutionist, then became president of the French Republic, and finally the ruler of the Second Empire. Rain makes him arrogant, conceited, cunning, evasive, and cowardly. His scenes are short, but Rains brings them to life.

There was some criticism of John Garfield's Porfirio Diaz at the time and since, with the main argument being that Garfield's demeanour was too modern and New York-naturalistic for historical roles, but his great acting and powerful personality triumphed over any anachronistic flavour. Montague Love, Gale Sondergaard (wonderfully subtle and serpentine as the manipulating Empress Eugenie), the brilliant and sturdy Harry Davenport as the emperor's doctor, and John Miljan, the energetic Joseph Calleia, and Irving Pichel are among the great actors in Juarez.

Gilbert Roland is moving and steadfast as a committed Mexican officer to the Emperor. Roland told me about Juarez on the set of a film he was making in 1964. "There was a feeling of importance, of excitement to it," he told me. "Even while we were shooting it, William Dieterle guided us all so expertly and with such flow and movement in the scenes that when I saw it complete, with Korngold's score and all, in a movie house, I got identically the feeling I had in the hurly-burly of acting in it."

Though Davis and Brian Aherne play the deep and profoundly committed marital love that Maximilian and Carlotta actually felt for one another, they got along like oil and water in real life. Both made digs at the other in their memoirs. They were clearly neither chemically or mentally compatible. Davis stated he was pompous, self-centred, and touchy, and that when she told him he should always wear a beard (which she intended as a complement), he stared down at her with disdain and told her she should always wear a black wig.

In various interviews I conducted with Aherne in the 1960s and 1970s, he spoke dismissively of Davis. "She was gifted, but she relied too much on her natural talent," he frowned. "It took a strong director who knew what he was getting himself into to rein her in and teach her discipline and control." She had a tendency to overdo everything, tearing emotions to bits. She didn't seem to understand the value of subtle understatement, of indirection." Given that

Aherne, as Davis herself always maintained, was not averse to hamming it up grandiloquently when the situation demanded it, his criticisms smacked of the pot calling the kettle black. Always terrified and offended by pushy women, Aherne married the shy, reserved (or so she was at the time) Joan Fontaine, who in real life was much like the anxious, frightened girl she portrayed so well in her starring breakthrough picture, Rebecca. (Later in life, Fontaine developed into a fiercely independent, confrontational personality, and her opinions about the male supremacy-inclined Aherne were not complimentary.)

Davis's lone recorded remark regarding the Aherne-Fontaine marriage was, "I don't know how she stands his uppity, supercilious ways."

It's fun to imagine how Davis and the legendary Paul Muni would have interacted if they had ever starred in the same scene in Juarez. Since Bordertown, both have come a long way. Muni, like Davis, went on to costume iconic films such as The Story of Louis Pasteur (for which he won an Oscar in 1936) and The Life of Emile Zola. Muni was regarded as "Mr. Warner" by the Warners by 1939. Everyone except his closest friends and his attentive, strong-willed wife called him "Muni." Even Hal Wallis and Jack Warner felt more at ease connecting with the Great One through intermediaries and messages. John Huston, who despised Muni's brother-in-law's influence with the Juarez screenplay, regarded him as tough in debate, winning not so much intellectually or logically as by sheer tenacity. When Muni was defeated in an argument, he simply stood firm and threatened to leave the project, which, according to Huston, "sent everybody scurrying and conciliating to beat the band."

Nonetheless, there is no doubting Muni's Juarez's overwhelming power. His inclination to conceal his own nature beneath the makeup, mannerisms, and general mystique of the man he was portraying in Juarez gave him a reality, verisimilitude, and persuasive force of character that viewers found captivating and irresistible. Muni enters a town square alone in his carriage in one of his most majestic images, with enemy soldiers all around him and a populace in thrall to his disloyal competitor. He goes to the palace door, forces his cowardly opponent out, and harangues the mob, winning their renewed devotion and the murder of his competitor against all odds. And he is quite moving when he laments Abraham Lincoln's death while banished in a mountain enclave surrounded by his few followers.

Juarez reflects highly on everyone involved in its creation. Donald Crisp, who played Bazaine, the commander of the French forces in Mexico, said Juarez was one of Hollywood's most underappreciated films, praising its epic sweep, amazing human variation, and vivid atmosphere.

"William Dieterle," Crisp recalled, "was a really gifted director who could capture the essentials of a historical film; he blended the characters, the action, the atmosphere into a colourful, authentic overall look that reminded me of Griffith at his best." Crisp, who had worked with Griffith in the early days and played General Grant in Birth of a Nation and the villain in Broken Blossoms, knew what he was talking about. "Dieterle made you care about the characters in Juarez; he had you rooting for one, then the other; it was a triumph of deeply felt empathy." He brought those characters to life, going above and beyond what was written about them in the script. It was an honour to work on a Dieterle film."

"Most of the acting is on a superlatively high level," observed James Shelley Hamilton of Juarez in The National Board of Review Magazine. "The contrasts in appearance, manner, and speech between Paul Muni as the stolid Indian and Brian Aherne as the elegant and refined Emperor are remarkably effective." When it comes to Bette Davis, Hamilton said, "[She] subdues her strikingly individual characteristics to a portrayal of the Empress Carlotta that is not only touching but over toned with premonitions of her eventual tragedy, and her finally flitting away into the darkness of madness is the most unforgettable moment in the picture."

13.

Bette Davis: Survivor

AFTER "MAKING DO" with several television projects to keep the money coming in, Davis came across a script that she felt would definitively end her horror-film cycle.

Connecting Rooms is known as the Mystery Film in the Bette Davis canon. It was never released in America, had a limited release in England, and has yet to be seen on American television, let alone on video cassettes or cable. I was one of the few people who saw this picture in England in 1971, thanks to a friend who arranged for a screening-room viewing.

In the spring of 1969, Pinewood Studios shot Connecting Rooms. For unknown reasons, the British publication was delayed until 1972. While it is far from one of Davis's best pictures, it also does not deserve to be at the bottom of her list. It should be seen in art houses now, some twenty years later, and would very probably do better on television and videocassettes than other commonly seen Davis pictures that are inferior to it.

In retrospect, it's simple to see why Davis chose Connecting Rooms. She felt it was a welcome change of pace after the grotesqueries of The Anniversary, and she was correct. It was produced by two Englishmen, Harry Field and Arthur Cooper, and was based on

Marion Hart's play of the same name, with script and direction by Franklin Collings.

The producers sealed the deal with Davis, who had been considering the script for two years, by enlisting Sir Michael Redgrave, a prominent stage and screen actor, to co-star with her. Each admired the other and had long desired to collaborate. Once dragged into it, Davis and Redgrave found themselves in accord with the script's flaws. It was often melodramatic, emotional, and unconvincing. A depressing narrative about the residents of a dingy London boarding home, it stars Davis as a middle-aged cellist who survives by performing in front of theatres. Sir Michael plays a former schoolteacher who was fired after being accused of having a gay romance with an attractive student protégé. Alexis Kanner, a young, gorgeous pop artist, song writer, and would-be gigolo, played the third lead. Davis develops an emotional attachment to Kanner and befriends her next-door neighbour, Redgrave. Despite his charm, Kanner is a cynical, opportunistic character, and Davis ends up with Redgrave when Kanner unkindly exposes his background.

Davis, whose cello work was impersonated by Ian Fleming's sister, Amaryllis, is modest, gentle, and well-intentioned in this. After playing horror-film grotesques and one-eyed harridans, she obviously thought that a sympathetic, warm character in the vein of The Sisters and All This and Heaven Too was in order. In this case, however, she did not have the skilled Anatole Litvak to lead her—only the insecure Franklin Gollings, who spent the whole of the film acting terrified of her. This "scaredy-cat" approach annoyed her greatly, and she quickly found herself brutally abusing the helpless Gollings. "I was rousing him to tell me what to do, for God's sake!"" She later stated. "I despise directors who don't direct!" Things would have gone better if Gollings had stood up to her even once-but he didn't. He even fainted on the scene once, out of sheer stress and the worse for wear after an unexpected drink or two. This infuriated her even more.

Davis and Redgrave spent a lot of time in her dressing room blue-pencilling and revising the script, and when the results were brought to Gollings, he hemmed and hawed indecisively.

Then there was the issue of Alexis Kanner, a young woman. Kanner, who was sassy and tactless, had an unwavering trust in the power of his own charm and photogenic abilities, and it was clear that he was not impressed with the Great Bette Davis. Soon, the two were shouting noisily, and Davis began looking for a replacement after thrusting him at Gollings and insisting that he be fully rehearsed. "She came up with that, not us!""Harry Field later explained. "She just took matters into her own hands without consulting us, even directing a scene when Gollings passed out once." She wanted Keith Baxter to take over for Kanner, but we had to tell her he wasn't young enough (the kid was supposed to be in his late teens), and she grumbled.

Much of Connecting Rooms is heartfelt and genuine. Davis and Redgrave use true, honest acting to make the mediocre material look better than it is. Davis seemed to restrain her typical tendency to overact, possibly influenced by co-star Vanessa Redgrave's subtler, more subdued style. Redgrave is moving as a man who feels unjustly buffeted by fate, and Kanner is so masculinely charismatic as the gigolo-like young heel that it's amazing he didn't get more work after that. Kanner reportedly told an interviewer, "If working with Bette Davis is what movies are all about, then I don't want any more of them!""

The film has its strong points as a study of loneliness and emotional anguish. It is too emotional at times, the tempo slows, and there is an excessive drabness, yet despite these flaws, it deserved an American release and greater distribution.

When Davis aged sixty-three in 1971, she faced yet another failure in Bunny O'Hare (previously known as Bunny and Billy). Davis was fascinated by the story and thought the job would suit her, but it was again another example of her poor judgement during this time.

Producer-director Gerd Oswald, who had directed her for television, and American-International entrepreneurs James H. Nicholson and Samuel Z. Arkoff had sold her on a narrative by Stanley Cherry, which Cherry and Coslough Johnson had developed into a script a few months before. They had also solicited the assistance of Davis's former Catered Affair co-star, Ernest Borgnine. Davis stated that she liked Borgnine and would be delighted to work with him again.

The plot revolves around a widow (Davis) who, when her home is foreclosed on by a bank, begins robbing similar establishments with the assistance of a previous bankrobber (Borgnine). The widow wishes to continue supporting her wretched, naive, dependent children (Reva Rose and John Astin) in this manner. The bank robber and lady proceed to careen about harsh New Mexico areas on a motorcycle, wreaking various mayhem and wearing wacky hippie clothes (the film's commercial text claimed they were the elderly response to Warren Beatty and Faye Dunaway's Bonnie and Clyde four years before).

Cop Jack Cassidy and criminologist Joan Delaney are on the trail of Borgnine and Davis. Cassidy despises hippies, especially elderly ones, and pursues them relentlessly, but the pair are acquitted by chance. Davis shucks off her children with the words "Fuck 'em!" at the end of the film.", as well as Borgnine being discovered as a supplier of toilets to low-income Chicanos. Many of Davis's followers questioned why she, who claimed to be concerned about good taste and high standards, would ever resort to four-letter words and filthy circumstances, and she herself felt guilty for making the picture since she had allowed the bad language and vulgar dénouement.

Davis and Borgnine began the film amicably enough, but according to Gerd Oswald, they soon began approaching him separately, requesting that situations be built up to their particular advantages. It was also mentioned that as Borgnine and Davis were forced to careen down New Mexico highways on the motorcycle, he didn't take special care to ensure her safety as she clutched to him furiously. Davis was enraged by everything, including the harsh sun, which irritated her skin, the strange New Mexico weather, which alternated between icy cold and unbearably hot, and the ludicrous, unbelievable situations that a frantic Oswald tried to hype up from the foolish, poorly motivated screenplay in which he, the stars, and everyone else had lost faith.

Back in Hollywood, Arkoff and Nicholson were receiving frantic phone calls and telegrams from the director, the stars, the cameraman (who was attempting to film the chaos in widescreen and Movielab Color), and even some prop people, who threatened to file a union complaint about the impossible working conditions on location.

Davis yelled and vowed to sue the corporation after seeing the first rough cut, claiming that they had chopped all sense out of the plot. Davis dropped her much-publicised legal threats after some alterations and additional recutting, claiming that Bunny O'Hare was a lost cause and she wanted to forget it and go on. Variety called it "a swift kick in the moviola," while the New York Post called it "weak" and "let her down," adding, "I don't know how they sold her on it in advance."

Following that, Dino De Laurentiis persuaded Davis to fly from California to Italy to create The Scientific Cardplayer (Lo Scopone Scientifico), also known as The Game. Alberto Sordi, a well-known Italian comedian, would appear beside her.

The endeavour was doomed from the outset. Davis did not get along with Sordi because, despite speaking excellent English, he insisted on shouting at her in staccato Italian. She believed it was a ruse to frighten her and show her who was boss, so she gave it her all, yelling some of her finest curses at him. She never apologised for her actions, remarking angrily, "What good would it have done, for Christ's sake?" Except for Sordi, who was bluffing, they would have had no idea of English civilities or my curses!"

The plot revolves around an egomaniacal American millionaire who likes regular card games with impoverished Italians hoping to gain a fortune from her. Of course, she rigs everything such that she is always the winner, but hope lives on in the hearts of her Italian suckers, and the game continues indefinitely. The Variety critic threw her a critical posy, writing, "Bette Davis dominates with a neat display of egomania and cruelty beneath a stance of gracious dignity." Silvana Mangano is one of her opponents at the perennial card game known as Scopa, and she nearly beats her numerous times. Finally, one of the enraged Italian teenagers presents her with a poison-filled cake. It's clear she won't be returning to her customary sport.

Joseph Cotten reprised his role as Davis's faithful friend who toys with her and makes ruefully subtle remarks. Sordi is efficient in his usual manner, and Silvana Mangano gives a lively performance as the card-game opponent.

In 1986, I saw the film at the Museum of Modern Art, where it was well received. The film reportedly made money in Italy (primarily due to Sordi's name), but received little distribution in both England and America, which is surprising given that the Eastman colour is beautiful, the production values are adequate, and the direction by Luigi Comencini extracts everything good from the Rodolfo Sonego script.

Davis, on the other hand, disliked the film, noting not only Sordi's rudenesses and prima-donna posturings, but also the fact that she had no idea the dialogue would be shot in Italian with dubbing.

Joseph Cotten, who subsequently claimed he only did the film because he adored Bette and wanted the money, believed she was not treated with respect, and that Sordi was seen as the star by the Italian cast and crew, while Davis was treated as a cameo player. Her part is significant, and although being restricted to a wheelchair, she manages to transmit kinetic energy and a sense of mobility. It's an unusual blend of the surreal and the actual, and it's not always successful, but the Italianate setting adds flavour and spice, so Davis doesn't need to apologise for Scientific Cardplayer.

Sordi told multiple interviewers that he didn't want to work with Davis again since she was always unpleasant to him and accused him of greedily hogging the camera. He tried, he said, to make light of her lack of tact, but this just served to enrage Davis even more. "Then I gave up," he explained.

Davis's friendship with actor Robert Wagner extended back to the early 1970s. He had used his clout to cast her in an episode of his television show, To Catch a Thief. In "A Touch of Magic," Davis portrayed a safecracker who took on various aliases. She pretended to be a fragile convalescent, then a magnificent lady, and finally a nun's "drag" and a hilarious schtick. She credited Wagner with convincing the writer to expand her role in order to showcase her variety.

Davis was saddened when Wagner's marriage to Natalie Wood ended, but happy when they remarried a few years later. Natalie was, as she frequently stated, "another daughter" to her. (Davis had previously appeared with her in The Star.)

Then, in 1972, Robert Wagner came to her aid once more. She co-starred with him in Madame Sin, a TV pilot that was later distributed in European theatres.

She is a sinister-looking, completely malevolent half-Chinese woman who engages in unending manipulations in this. Ensconced in a Scottish castle that, as one reviewer put it, "is loaded with typical spy-movie gadgetry," she comes into conflict with the Wagner character, who is eager to foil her schemes. "Evil genius (Davis) uses former C.I.A. agent (Wagner) as a pawn for control of Polaris submarine," one critic wrote. The elaborate performance ends with Bad defeating Good; with Bette in charge, it's well worth seeing."

Davis is dark and sinuous, dressed in a gaudy black wig, snappy black gown, and jangling jewellery. Her poisonously powerful performance received positive feedback both at home and abroad.

Davis had been appearing on television since the early 1950s. She never took them seriously, but she did occasionally get good parts on Wagon Train, Perry Mason, and other shows. Many were done as pilots that were never picked up as series.

Two of her television films from 1972-1973 demonstrate the calibre of her work in that medium. Davis supplied a satirical, funny picture of an eccentric jurist who chooses to create a detective agency and hires an ex-con as her partner in The Judge and Jake Wyler. They work together to solve the murder of a businessman. The plot features clever twists, and Davis performs with a light, throwaway style that is rare for her, however the old overdone, occasionally hammy Davis mannerisms did appear when director David Lowell Rich wasn't looking. Doug McClure and Joan Van Ark were excellent supporters. Later, Davis told an interviewer, McClure was "all man and very cute."

The Judge and Jake Wyler, like so many of her other television appearances, was intended to be a pilot for a series, but footage was added to make it a full length film, which debuted as a TV Movie of the Week for NBC in December 1972. "Bette was always a good sport in the television shows she was forced to make because she needed money or had nothing else on tap," Kent Smith, who played a supporting part in it, told me. I was there to witness her create something out of nothing with the Judge. Even in drek, she always went all out. That was all part of her professionalism."

Scream, Pretty Peggy, a 78-minute 1973 television film, received the following criticism from William Schoell, author of the book Stay Out of the Shower on horror films: "[The picture] is a ridiculous rip-off of Psycho that has yet another crazed cross-dresser as the killer." To believe it, you must see Ted Bessell galloping around in drag. The plot revolves around a college girl who works as a housekeeper in a property with a horrible secret. To put it mildly, Jimmy Sangster's screenplay is absurd, Gordon Hessler's direction never rises beyond the ordinary, and Bette Davis as Bessell's mother doesn't put herself out too much."

Bette Davis began doing a one-woman show, a sort of retrospective of her life and career, in 1973. Her debut performance at Town Hall in New York was such a success that she brought it all across the country, including Australia and Europe.

The evening's schedule never changed. The first half was a collection of film clips carefully chosen by film historians such as Don Koll. Davis spent the second half fielding personal and professional sallys and questions.

These meetings drew a huge number of gay men, who enjoyed her reminiscences and humorous, sharp observations about previous coworkers, as well as her complicated relationships with Miriam Hopkins and Joan Crawford. At the 1973 Town Hall event, Michael Ritzer, then a reporter for Quirk's Reviews, stunned Bette and the crowd when he stood up and informed her that Beyond the Forest had always been his favourite film. Davis shot him one of her steely stares and snorted, "Oh really. .," to which the audience erupted in laughter. Surprisingly, Ritzer was a trailblazer in his assessment of

Beyond the Forest, which has since become a cult classic.

Davis was really nice during the tour. She answered as many questions (prepared and pre-sorted) as time and energy allowed. She re-enacted the two-cigarette scene in Now, Voyager, told Miriam what a b*tch she was during The Old Maid shoot, and refused to confess that William Wyler was the only man she truly loved but refused to surrender to. She recited the get-ready-for-a-bumpy-night speech from All About Eve until it ran out of her ears, praised Eddie Goulding and Willie Wyler as her favourite directors, talked about her feuds with Jack Warner, marriages, fellow actors like Charles Boyer, Leslie Howard, Paul Henreid, and her favourite-of-favourites, Claude Rains.

Before embarking on this tour, Davis had featured in a Town Hall series called "Legendary Ladies," among three other luminaries: Sylvia Sidney, Myrna Loy, and Joan Crawford, each having her own evening. Bette kept a civil tongue about Joan because they were both working on the same project under the same umbrella, and Crawford reciprocated, but many thought the series would have been more vibrant if the ladies had let loose on each other. Davis was more forthright later, when she was on her own, but still reserved for her. She remembered telling the press in 1962 that before What Ever Happened to Baby Jane? No bank would take a chance on a film featuring "two old broads" like her and Crawford, and Crawford had sent her a scathing note warning her not to speak to her in that manner again.

Like many others, I am intrigued by what appears to be a Bette Davis and Joan Crawford infatuation among many gay males. Despite the fact that the formal and caustic Davis image is easily mimicked, Crawford, like Judy Garland, has gained a cult following. But it was the Crawford-Davis gay cult phenomena that I was interested in, and I wrote an analytical piece about it for Quirk's Reviews in 1973.

Joan Crawford remarked after reading "The Cult of Bette and Joan," as I termed it, that she wasn't sure what the gays saw in her, though she had an easier time understanding the gay fixation on Davis. We discussed the subject thoroughly over supper one evening at her place.

Joan began by adding that she and her friends had found "The Cult of Bette and Joan" to be both hilarious and sharp, and recalled Leonard Frey, who played Harold in the 1970 film version of The Boys in the Band, holding up my 1968 book, The Films of Joan Crawford, in full view of the camera. Joan noted that gays were great people, that she had many gay friends, and that she was pleased to join Garland and Davis in their pantheon of goddesses, but she was unsure whether she deserved to be included.

I stated that many homosexual men are associated with Joan's and Bette's struggle—for careers, for men, for self-respect, for social acceptability, for all the good things in life, as portrayed in their 1930s–1950s movies. I pointed out the marketing for their movies, for instance: "Bette Davis as a Twelve O'Clock Girl in a Nine O'Clock Town" (Beyond the Forest). "No One Can Hold a Candle to Joan Crawford When Joan Is Carrying the Torch" (Good-bye, My Fancy). "It Happens in the Best of Families but Who Would Have Thought It Could Happen to Her?" (Now, Voyager). "Joan's Having Man-Trouble Again!" (Daisy Kenyon). "Disillusioned, Sick with Men, Does Joan Dare Love Once More?" (Humoresque). "She's Meanest When She's Lovin' Most!" (Jezebel). "Deep in her heart, she knew she'd never be able to hold him!""The Corn Is Green." "He strayed, and he paid-she took care of that!"" (On-Demand Payment).

Then I described the standard Bette and Joan plots with which many gay men identified: Joan climbing, on a ladder of rich and powerful men, from rags to riches (Sadie McKee); Bette determined to break out of the stultifying small town to glamour and men in Chicago (Beyond the Forest); Joan, unrequitedly and obsessively in love with a guy, goes bonkers and shoots him to death when he takes up with someone else (Possessed); Bette and Miriam fighting over men with both of them losing out (Old Acquaintance); Joan suffering unrequited love for a loser, winding up in a house of ill fame, then going for a smash finish as the wife of the richest guy in town (Flamingo Road); Bette defying the conventional monster-mother to go out and fight for happiness and love (Now, Voyager); good Bette and bad Bette in a dual role as twins fighting over a guy, who—for a while-prefers the frosted naughty girl to the unfrosted goody-goody (A Stolen Life); Joan on the rags to riches shtick again, loving a no-good son of a bitch and winding up with a squeaky-clean boy scout (Mannequin).

Joan stated at the end of the performance that she recognized her and Davis' attractiveness to gay males. Davis, for her part, frequently stated that gays were among her audience's most appreciative, tasteful, and artistically savvy members. She admired their devotion to her, which was, admittedly, overbearing at times. According to a common Greenwich Village joke, two gay men are drinking in a pub when one of them says to the other, "You must be in love with Bette Davis the way you go on about her at such length!"" The other responds, "I'm madly in love with Bette Davis!" Bette Davis, I AM!"

Davis noted on her tour that she enjoyed seeing nightclub comedians, drag queens, and others mock her, but that she could do it better herself. She would then proceed to illustrate by smoking, twitching her pelvis, bulging her eyes, and flailing her elbows. She insisted that she had never stated, "Petah-the Lettah!"" in any image. It was actually a combination of two of her films, The Letter and In This Our Life, in which she drives a guy named Peter (Dennis Morgan) to suicide.

Bette Davis, at the age of sixty-six, was given a great opportunity in 1974, one she cherished-but it ended in disaster. In show business circles, there is still controversy over whether Davis was a victim or culprit of what became known as "the Miss Moffat mess."

Davis had wished to play the heroic Welsh school teacher in The Corn Is Green for thirty years. Though the film (made in 1944) was a hit, she believed that, at thirty-six, she had been too young for the character, considering that Ethel Barrymore, its original, had been sixty-one when she portrayed it on Broadway. Longtime admirer and skilled director and writer Joshua Logan approached her with the notion of a musical version to be toured and sent to Broadway. Mary Martin had been the original candidate for the role, but she had declined at the last time. Emlyn Williams penned the words, Albert Hague the music.

Davis informed Logan that her Two's Company musical attempt of 1952–1953 had "left a bad taste" in her mouth; she didn't think she was up to it. She cheered up when Logan told her that he was transferring the story from Wales to the Deep South and that the race question would be dealt four-square by making Morgan Evans a black youngster of rare intelligence whom Miss Moffat's guidance encourages to future greatness.

Delighted with the update of the topic, confident that the musical score and lyrics would be suited to her restricted abilities, and that dance would be modest and discreet, Davis took the bait.

The trouble started right away. She had trouble remembering lines. Dorian Harewood, a young black actor-singer whose big break this would have been, was nervous trying to deal with her wild, unpredictable approach, and they didn't get along. She fell from stress in Philadelphia, finding little solace in the knowledge that advance ticket purchases in New York insured that the show would run for at least a year.

Josh Logan and Davis came from the flop as bitter adversaries. "She was tactless, overbearing, and did not blend in with the cast," he stated, and, in his opinion, manufactured a series of illnesses to avoid her obligation. She startled her cast by abruptly pausing the action to protest about a scene. She threw young Harewood off by failing to recognize his indications. Davis went to bed in a Philadelphia hotel after experiencing sore throats, neuralgic aches, and hysteria. Then she said that a back injury sustained in a fall in 1957 had flared again. Logan went to her room and was flanked by two physicians, a lawyer, and an insurance representative. He almost accused her of feigning illness and then implored her to show some professionalism, some regard for the cast of young aspirants, notably the despondent Harewood, whose destiny she was "mangling beyond the point of return." Angered, Davis summoned her own team of doctors, who advised Logan that he was dealing with an elderly woman who had no business being in such a stressful situation, and that if she continued, she might die in his hands. Logan, a director of many Broadway hits, had a history of mental breakdowns, and he warned his wife Nedda Harrigan that "the Wicked Witch of the West," as he called Davis, might well bring on "the grand extravaganza nervous breakdown of my life," insisting angrily that Davis was exaggerating her various afflictions to cop out."" he explained. Davis ignored all appeals and withdrew at a cost of hundreds of thousands of dollars. Logan ended the performance and never forgave her. Davis took a leave of absence. She rested for the majority of 1975, despite persistent reports about her health, and she was soon ready for more action. But, she told the reporters, she would never, ever go back to the theatre!

14.

The Lioness in Winter

AS OF 1989 Davis was frequently featured in the media. Her appearance remained a source of concern, as her face appeared ghoulishly skeletal beneath the excessive makeup and bright blond wig. The honours kept pouring, including a Kennedy Center tribute in late 1987, which she felt had been withheld for years due to her liberal Democratic beliefs. (Whenever they sent her a questionnaire asking for her opinion on a winner, she always replied, "Me!") In summer 1988, she managed to take off to the Villa d'Este in northern Italy, where she scooped up yet another award for her creative achievements at Campione Casino, near Lake Como, in between clashes with Larry Cohen over Wicked Stepmother. The Film Society of Lincoln Center finally honoured her in April 1989 with a magnificent homage followed by a VIP party at Tavern on the Green. Earlier in 1989, she was recognized at the American Cinema Awards in Hollywood, alongside Clint Eastwood and Julio Iglesias, to benefit the Motion Picture Country Home and Hospital. She briefly fainted in front of her friends and followers at her last occasion. Liz Smith reported that after decades of friendship, she had now joined longtime friend Olivia De Havilland to her long list of adversaries because Olivia had "upstaged" her when she received a French government homage in 1987. A more foreboding tone was struck when a tabloid detailed her ailments: a hip that had failed to heal properly and kept her in constant pain; a sapping of her strength that had her wondering if she could ever work again; her disappointment over not receiving solid job offers; and her dashed hopes of playing cosmetician Helena Rubinstein, a role she insisted she was "born" to create.

Davis' isolation from her family (totally estranged from B.D.; friendly but distant with Michael in distant Boston) persisted. Margot was essentially out of thought and out of mind by then, Gary's duty, with him paying Lochland School $15,000 each year for her care. To a point, her apartment, with its mementos and New England furnishings, remained a West Hollywood gathering place for friends and fans, but as one friend put it, "she's not even tending to her patio garden anymore, something that used to give her so much pleasure... she's gotten to the point where she's almost unreachable." She isn't interested in anyone."

The friend went on to say, "It's like she's holed up in her house just waiting to die." The cancer that was slowly killing her went unmentioned in the public press.

She remained close to daughterly and faithful Kathryn Sermak, but recognized that Kathryn had a life of her own at thirty-three. As a result, she kept the reins loose. She had learnt the hard way the truth of Mrs. Aphra Behn's famous lines: "I hold my love but lightly, for things with wings held tightly, want to fly."

Those who watched and waited believed Bette Davis' thoughts were frequently focused on the lovely place in Forest Lawn where Ruthie and Bobby lay. Two of the four men who had caused her so much anguish (Ham Nelson and Arthur Farnsworth) had died before her.

The gorgeous young guys she sought even in her sixties were now only distant recollections. Despite being hurt by them, she insisted until the end that it was better to lead with one's heart and be wounded than to close up and withdraw, because doing so meant death.

She still had supporters, but their passion, perseverance, and preoccupation with her and her mythology had taken on the quality of a story that had been told too many times. Friends stayed to the end, but they couldn't completely penetrate her ever-deepening seclusion, that profound aloneness she had anticipated for herself as her final chapter decades earlier.

But there would be one last hurrah. She departed Hollywood in September 1989 for the 37th San Sebastian International Film Festival, where she was to receive an award. Her attorney, Harold

Schiff, later informed the public that the breast cancer she had been battling since her 1983 mastectomy had recurred, was metastasizing, and was deadly. "The doctors said," he went on to say, "let her go on going about her business."

Davis's close friend, Hollywood Reporter columnist Robert Osborne, agreed with her wish to put on a brave front for the press and public. He paraphrased her as saying in his September 1 column, "I hope this will prove to the world that I'm not dying." All those horrible tales and rumours about how sick I'm supposed to be are the only thing making me sick. Where do they begin? And how can you make them stop?"

The New York Post's film critic, V. A. Musetto, was in San Sebastian on September 22 and characterised her as "a tiny, pencil-thin old woman who had trouble walking unassisted." She still had the unmistakable appearance of a Hollywood queen. She appeared from her automobile in front of the Victoria Eugenia Theater, dressed in a sequined purple gown. The noises of police firing tear gas at protesters, who in turn were throwing bottles and rocks at the cops, could be heard in the background. The citizens of San Sebastian, on the other hand, paid little attention to the street fighting, which is becoming a routine occurrence in this hotbed of the Basque separatist movement.

"Besides," he continued, "Their minds were really on that fragile 81-year-old woman."

"Bette! Bette!" The Spaniards' yelling was evident to everyone present: music to her ears. Inside the cinema, blowing frantically on her cigarette, she spread her arms and cried back, despite the obvious effort required, "Muchas gracias! Thank you very much!"

The following night, when she presented Andrei Konchalovsky with a festival award for his picture Homer and Eddie, the director made a gesture that pleased the audience. To accept, he got down on his knees in front of her. Onlookers later said that this spontaneous expression of his admiration seemed to move her deeply.

During another news conference, "more than 400 of the world's journalists gave her a standing ovation," according to Musetto. She informed the assembled reporters that she liked her job and that she wanted to act all the time. Dark Victory, Jezebel, Now, Voyager, All About Eve, and What Ever Happened to Baby Jane were among her favourite roles. She didn't like Ronald Reagan as an actor, but she thought he was "very good" as president and "made us all very patriotic." "If I had met him way, way back, he would never have escaped me," she said of her Right of Way co-star Jimmy Stewart, "but it's too late now." Although she was nice with Joan Crawford, she referred to another co-star, Miriam Hopkins, as a "bitch." It's impossible to collaborate with." She despised the colorization of her previous films and described it as "heartbreaking." She also said Hollywood's recent films were "very sad."

She took off for Paris, elated by her Spanish reception, accompanied by devoted companion Kathy Sermak. People who saw her believed she was still agitating the dying embers of what had been a scorching, furnacelike eighty-one years. As she had always stated, old age was not for wimps. When she arrived in Paris, however, her strength had entirely abandoned her, and Kathy took her to the American Hospital.

She lingered for a while. Liz Smith and other well-informed columnists kept her condition private. She wanted to accomplish what she needed to do alone, away from reporters and other intruders.

"Accommodation to life's inescapable realities is not surrender," she had stated in London fifty-three years previously, at the age of twenty-eight, when she understood she would have to return to fulfil her Warner contract after the hard-fought court case she had lost. And, late on Friday, October 6, 1989, in Paris—three thousand miles from the city in Massachusetts where she was born eighty-one years previously, and six thousand miles from the Hollywood of her triumphs-Bette Davis, feisty and realistic to the last, accommodated.

When the news broke the next day, the press gave her a farewell that she would have been very proud of. She was front-page news, and the compliments were well-deserved.

Harold Schiff and Michael Merrill arranged for her corpse to be returned to Hollywood, where her funeral was held on October 12 at Forest Lawn Memorial Park, officiated by Reverend Robert M. Bock of the First Christian Church of North Hollywood. Only twenty-five family members and close friends attended the private service. The marble sarcophagus, inscribed DAVIS and containing a statue of a woman modelled after B.D.'s face and proportions, had already seen three interments. Bette, Ruthie, and Bobby had finally been reunited. Later, Kathryn Sermak, Robert Wagner, George Schaefer (who directed her in Right of Way) and others planned a big memorial service at a Warner Brothers lot sound stage attended by everyone in Hollywood who knew and loved Davis. Robert Osborne, a close friend, said, "It's no accident that [Bette] chose as her final resting place a plot of Forest Lawn that overlooks the Burbank Studios and all those soundstages where she churned out the good work for eighteen years."

Davis' will was published a month after she died. B.D., as well as Margot, were completely excluded. B.D.'s boys were likewise passed over. The estate, estimated to be worth between $600,000 and a million dollars, was split equally between Kathryn Sermak and Michael Merrill. Her niece Faye Forbes, childhood friend Robin Brown, and Mrs. Michael Merrill all received minor bequests. The widespread belief about Margot was that Davis had arranged for Michael to cover her bills. (Gary Merrill, Michael's father, who was in his seventies at the time, had been paying Margot's fees for years.) "Unfortunately, their mother chose to have them follow her rather than their hearts," Harold Schiff said, attempting to explain why Davis didn't include B.D. 's kids in her will. They'll say after twenty years, 'That was our grandmother; why didn't we know her?'"

B.D., who had until December 5 to contest the will, told reporters on November 7 that she had no plans to do so. Davis's only natural child, who now lives in Charlottesville, Virginia, where she trains Arabian horses, scoffed, "I would be shocked if [the will] mentioned me." "That's the way she is with everyone," she added with a grin, still referring to her mother in the present tense. Either she owns them or they are her adversaries." B.D. had frequently described her mother as "a totally destructive force in my children's and my life." When told that Davis' maid would have prohibited B.D. from attending the burial, she laughed and said she had no plans to go anyhow. B.D., no shrinking violet, went on Connie Chung's TV talk show to say that her mother had died years before for her, that she was a tremendous celebrity, certainly, but a star in private as well as public, and that she, B.D., had done her thing and her mother had done hers. "Nobody expected a movie queen to be an exemplary wife and mother-that was not her destiny," one fan remarked. Great artists follow their own set of rules. Bette Davis would have been a lot more content if she had never married or had children. She was a part of the planet. Her gifts were intended for the world, and she gave them to them with great charity". "She will never really die," wrote another fan. And it is correct. Bette Davis's vivid and unique mystique will keep her securely ensconced among the ever-creative living, owing to the magic of film.

Printed in Great Britain
by Amazon